With best wishes

Gary Chapman

October 2018

French Beaded Flowers in Sugar

Gary Chapman

French Beaded Flowers in Sugar

Gary Chapman

© Copyright Gary Chapman, Edditt Publishing, 2018

All rights reserved. No part of this publication may be reproduced, stored in a retrieval system, or transmitted in any form or by any means, electronic, mechanical, photocopying, recording or otherwise, without prior written permission of the publisher/author.

Paperback
ISBN 978-1-909230-31-6

Other formats available
ebook (Epub) ISBN 978-1-909230-32-3
ebook (Mobi) ISBN 978-1-909230-33-0

www.eddittpublishing.com

Contents

Author's Note
1-4 Introduction
5-6 Overview
7 Equipment
8-14 Things to Consider
15-20 Basic Formation
21-22 Wiring
23-24 Leaves
25-30 Simple, Single-Looped French Beaded Flowers
31-34 More Elaborate, Single-Looped French Beaded Flower
35-38 Single and Double-Looped French Beaded Flower
39-42 Single-Looped, Cluster French Beaded Flower
43-48 Coiled, Spiral French Beaded Flower
49-54 Daisy French Beaded Flower
55-58 Blossom French Beaded Flower
59-64 Fantasy Multi-Coloured Blossom French Beaded Flower
65-68 Gardenia or Magnolia French Beaded Flower
69-73 Blue Fantasy French Beaded Flower
74-78 Rose French Beaded Flower
79-84 Poppy French Beaded Flower
85-88 Sunflower French Beaded Flower
89-94 Peony French Beaded Flower
95-100 Dahlia French Beaded Flower

A Range of Other French Beaded Flowers in Sugar
About the Author
Book Adverts

Author's Note

I first became aware of French Beaded Flowers about twenty years ago and thought they looked extraordinarily different and beautiful. They became quite inspirational and for many years I had the idea of recreating them in sugar but how? After much thought and playing around with various ideas I had an epiphany during a class I was undertaking at Knightsbridge-PME in London when I was experimenting with the PME ribbed roller. Eventually, I was able to find more suitable and finer ribbed rollers, which I have used in this book to create the beaded effected on rolls of paste that form the petals of flowers and leaves.

It has been a lengthy and complicated journey to arrive at the French beaded flowers in sugar shown in this book. It is a totally new technique of creating sugar flowers and perhaps one that could not have been advanced and advocated until now following the trend for bigger flowers and for fantasy flowers and a greater acceptance of creating something different rather than just focusing on replicating natural flowers.

Lastly, I am also making an important statement with regard to plagiarism and copyright. My technique of recreating French Beaded Flowers in Sugar as seen in this book has been an original creation and subject to copyright. This new technique can be replicated for commercial cake making or for competition work, but I do not give anyone permission to use this technique for commercial gain in the form of real-life classes or demonstrations, magazine features or projects, online classes or any other online tutorial including youtube. Any attempt to use this technique on these platforms will be seen as breaking my copyright and subject to legal proceedings.

If photographs are uploaded anywhere using my technique they must be accompanied by the text 'based on the technique of French Beaded Flowers created by Gary Chapman as expressed in his book French Beaded Flowers in Sugar.'

Most of the cakes in this book have been painted with a variety of paint effects – an adaptation of some of the techniques used to paint and decorate walls for house décor. This is a technique I developed at the same time as fabric effects in the 1990s. Another book on these paint effects will be available. Details are at the end of the book.

Introduction

No-one knows with any certainty how and when the art of making flowers out of beads first came about. Beads made of stones, bones, pearls and shells were some of the first objects made by ancient man and used as personal adornment. However, the technology for glass bead making dates back 3,000 years to the ancient Egyptians and was expanded upon by the Romans. When Christianity took hold, personal adornment was frowned upon and there was a decline. From the 12th century, there was a revival of glass bead making in Venice and it was from here that beads were sent all over Europe primarily for religious use as rosaries but also as simple jewellery.

Allegedly, the art of making beaded flowers originated in the 16th century when they were formed into stunning arrangements for religious purposes in churches such as mourning wreaths and altar decorations. It was only later that it became fashionable to have them as home decorations and for wedding bouquets.

A wedding bouquet
reproduced courtesy of Lauren Harpster

Beads also became an essential ingredient in couture for French fashions perhaps as early as the 18th century when French dress designers added beads into their designs to incorporate into balls gowns.

The technique of making French beaded flowers that developed over centuries is characterized by its simplicity with the beads strung on wire and twisted into several basic patterns. Beaded flower arrangements were less expensive, available throughout the year and relatively durable. They were perfect during winter when fresh blooms were not available and didn't need watering or tending.

There was a resurgence in the usage of beads for fashion in the 1920s and 1930s and they were given prominence by Hollywood costume designers. At the same time, beaded flower arrangements were exported from Europe to America and sold in department stores along with kits to make your own flowers, complete with materials and patterns.

There was another resurgence in the 1960s with various people teaching and writing how-to-books about French bead flowers and now with arts and crafts being given more prominence, it has become even more popular today.

A bouquet of French beaded Dahliss
reproduced courtesy of Lauren Harpster

I have bought numerous books on the subject to try and understand how the flowers are made and then adapt and re-create them in sugar. This is the key – the flowers I have made in sugar are adaptations and I have taken numerous liberties and flights of fancy in my designs because of the constraint of working in sugar.

I have also been inspired by Lauren Harpster, a contemporary French beaded flower maker. Lauren is a wife, and mother based in the USA and is completely obsessed with French beaded flowers. She teaches how to make them through her website Lauren's Creations and publishes books in her French Beading Patterns series. She discovered French beading in 2011 when she was learning new bead weaving techniques and became quickly fascinated as it combined her love of flowers with a love of beads. Now she is proud to be one of those keeping the old art alive.

A bouquet of mixed French beaded flowers
reproduced couresy of Lauren Harpster

Take a look at Lauren's website at www.laurenscreations.net for a range of wonderful images and free beginner's tutorials along with patterns and tutorials available to purchase.

Overview
French Beaded Flowers in Sugar

My technique for creating the beads to form French beaded flowers in sugar relies on the simple idea of impressing a sheet of paste with a vertical, ribbed pattern by the use of ribbed rollers and then rolling up the paste and sealing it with sugar glue to create what looks like rolls of beads. The method of doing this is fully explained in the Basic Formation chapter.

Overview

Equipment

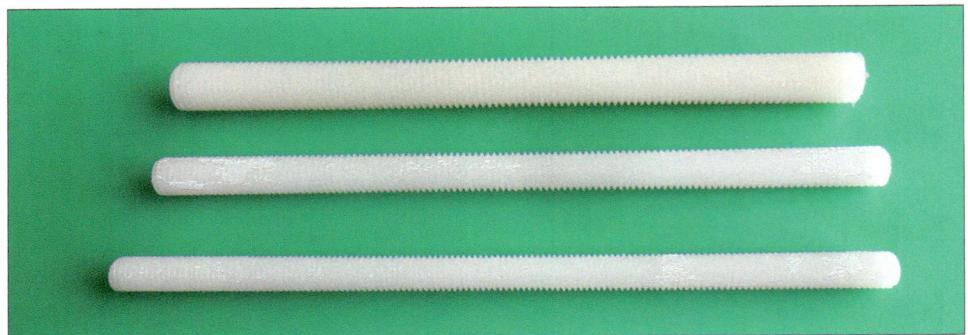

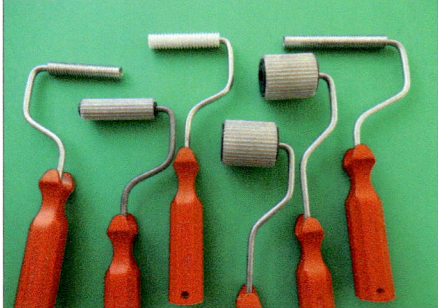

A range of tools are avaialble to create the lined or ribbed impression on the paste to form the beaded rolls. The best is a series of Nylon threaded studding (seen in three sizes at the top of the page and all 8" / 200mm in length). The sizes 8mm (M8), 10 mm (M10) and 12mm (M12) thread width are probably the best. These can be bought online in a variety of places including eBay.

Other interesting tools are shown on the right. These include at the top a range of rollers used in clay craft (with red handles). In the middle are metal threaded studding widely available in DIY stores and online and at the bottom the PME ribbed roller and the acrylic ribbed rollers used for smocking in cake decorating.

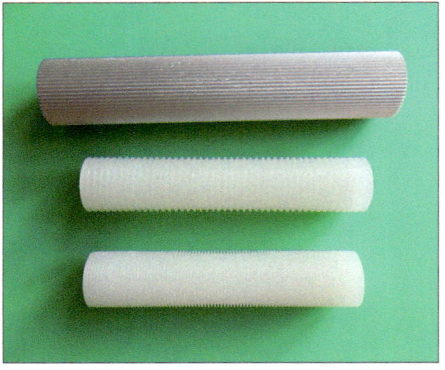

Things To Consider

Paste mix

First of all, let's look at the paste mix needed to make the French beaded flowers.

It is best to use just flower paste (gumpaste). Please note that ordinary sugarpaste or fondant will not work. The paste has to be stretchy with a robust texture, which you don't get by just using sugarpaste on it's own. I sometimes add a small amount of Renshaw's Extra fondant (sugarpaste) as I find it makes it slightly easier to work with.

You will have to experiment with your preferred brand and do remember that some brands of flowerpaste (gumpaste) are better than others. I prefer to use the Wilton gumpaste, Satin Ice gumpaste or the flower paste from a Piece of Cake in Thame, UK.

Sometimes there are problems with the paste. For example, on occasion when I have made one of the beaded rolls, they might split or fall apart when I manipulate them. In this instance, I add a small amount of tylose powder and allow the paste to settle before starting again. Sometimes I add some liquid glucose to soften the paste if it is too brittle.

The three brands I find particularly suitable for making the French beaded flowers are the Wilton Gum Paste, Satin Ice Gum Paste and the flowerpaste from a Piece of Cake in Thame.

No doubt many homemade flower pastes will also work as well as gelatin paste.

The thinness of working paste

An important thing to think about is how thick or thin to roll out your paste to make the basic roll to create the French beaded flowers.

If you roll out a thick sheet of paste you will produce a thick, larger roll, which may not look too good. A thinner, finer sheet of paste will produce neat, smaller rolls but you run the risk of splitting the paste when impressing the ribbed roller over the paste if it is too thin. So you have to practice first to achieve the optimum thickness.

Pasta Machine

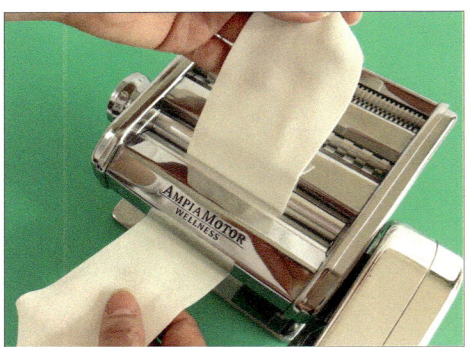

If you have a pasta machine, this will quickly produce even sheets of paste, which is invaluable in reducing the time it takes to start making the beaded rolls that will form the flowers and the leaves. An electric one is much easier to use than a hand-cranked one.

The pasta machine has many other applications for use in cake decorating and can, of course, be used for making pasta!

Stickiness

When rolling out a sheet of paste, use icing (powdered) sugar to stop any stickiness on the paste and fingers. You can sprinkle from an icing sugar shaker or keep a small bag of muslin or a bought bag to contain the icing sugar. Dabbing the icing sugar onto the surface of the paste or on your fingers will help reduce any stickiness.

Sugar glue

Sugar glue must be used to seal the rolls of beads. This glue is a useful 'sticking' agent and simple to make. Crumble small pieces of sugarpaste (rolled fondant) into a cup and add some water. Place in a microwave on high for a few seconds, repeating the process, until dissolved. You can adjust the density and thickness of the glue by adding more paste, if required.

Colour

Colour schemes are vital in making flowers. Don't be frightened of using colour and experiment. Most importantly, try to harmonise the colours that you use into your overall colour scheme and design for your cake. Significantly, colour can be used to great advantage in my beaded flowers by using alternate coloured layers or rows.

Dusting

Many flowers and leaves can benefit from dusting with lustre colours, and I use a range of dusting powders from various sources. I prefer to dust the flower after it has been created and dried. And, if dusting leaves, dust them before you assemble around the flower.

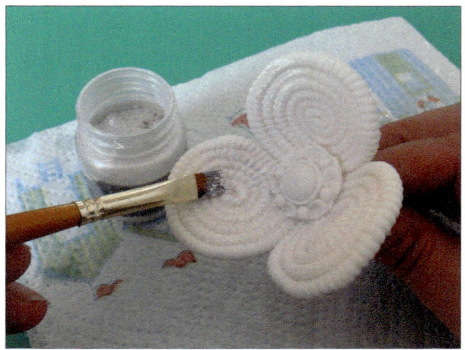

Steaming or Spraying With a Glaze

It is best to allow the flowers to dry first before steaming over a kettle or spraying with a glaze.

Flower Centres

Most of my French beaded flowers are created around a core flower centre on a ribbed cocktail stick and glued together with sugar glue.

Many different flower centres can be created (see opposite left), and most are made using a finer beaded roll to form beaded centres. They must be made and left to dry for several days before applying petals and leaves.

Some are simple loops – single, double, triple or a cluster. Others are small spirals. Some are created on a flattened cone that is dried before a spiral beaded roll is applied (used for daisies and sunflowers for example).

In others, a ball of paste is glued to a cocktail stick and dried and then vertical beads applied and glued (used for dahlias and one of my fantasy flowers).

Finally, jewelled centres can also be used – they also need to be dried and then painted or dusted. There are numerous jewel moumouldlds on the market with some wonderful designs.

Some centres are composites using a core jewelled centre with surrounding beaded roll loops.

Things to Consider

Using the Rollers

I tend to use three sizes of the nylon rollers as described earlier. The images below show each in terms of scale and the impression. The top shows the wider 12mm thread (M12), the middle 10mm thread (M10) and the bottom 8mm thread (M8). Remember the rollers do not dictate the size of the beaded roll. They provide varying sizes of thread. It is the thickness of the paste that determines the size of the beaded roll.

If a finer, more delicate impression is required for a beaded roll use the finer thread of 8mm (M8) and for a larger impression the 12mm thread (M12).

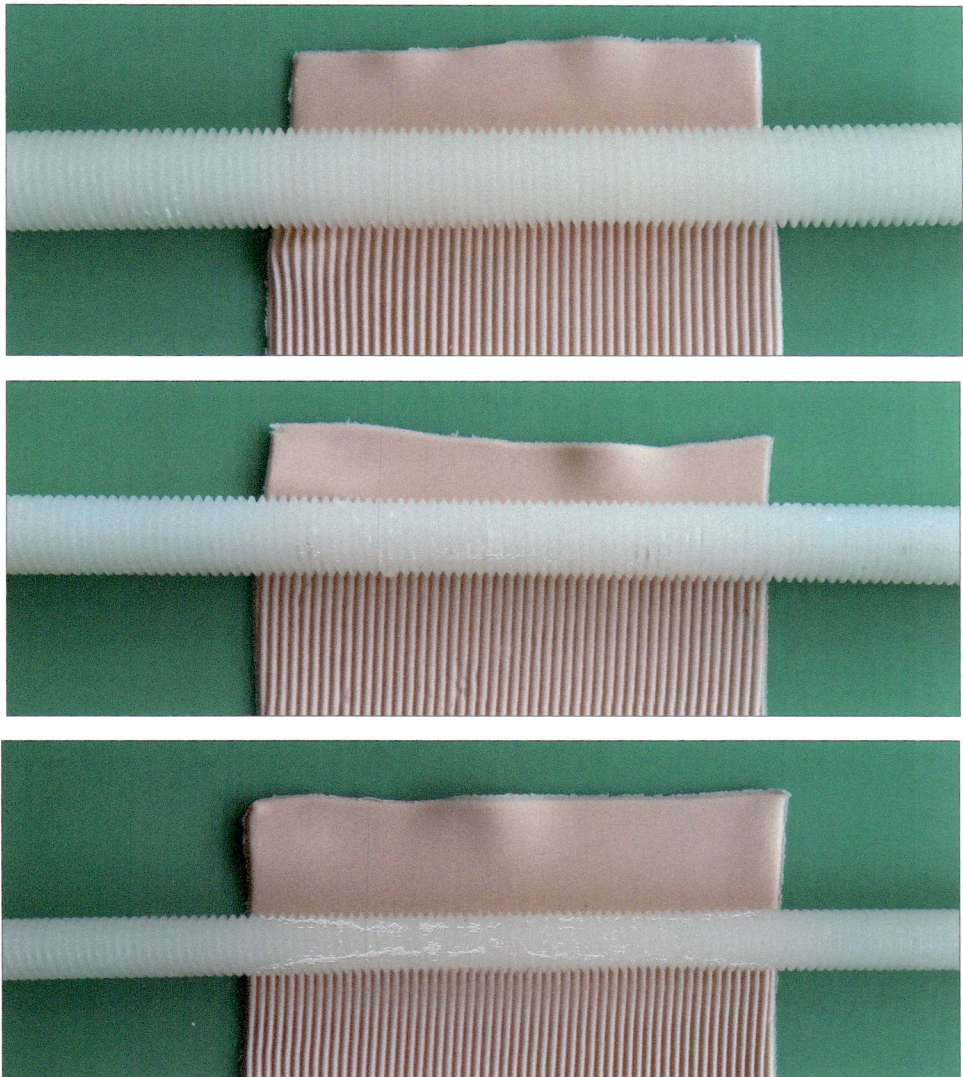

Size of the Beaded Rolls and Different Types of Beaded Rolls

Mostly, the beaded rolls are created roughly the same size for each flower, but the rolls can be of different thicknesses – see below showing five examples from thin and finer at the top getting bigger toward the bottom.

However, there are other variations shown below and on the right, which are useful for creating specific petal or leaf shapes. I have taken certain liberties to make these changes, and this latter approach is an adaptation of how to make real French beaded flowers modified explicitly to usage in sugar.

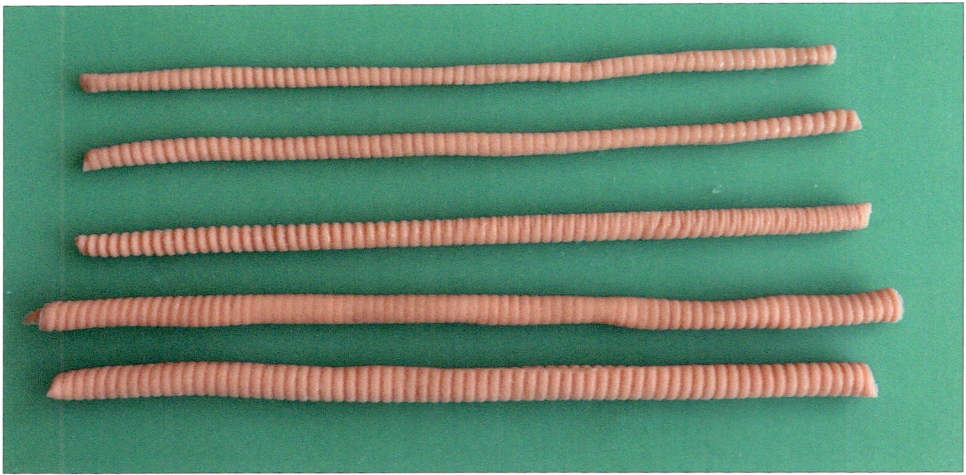

The arrangement below will create a petal or leaf that is fuller and fatter at the top and tapers at the base.

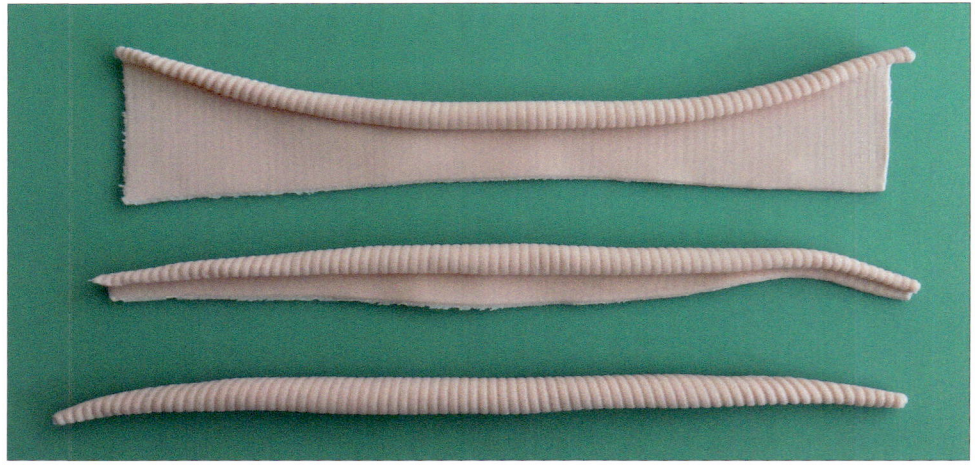

Things to Consider   14

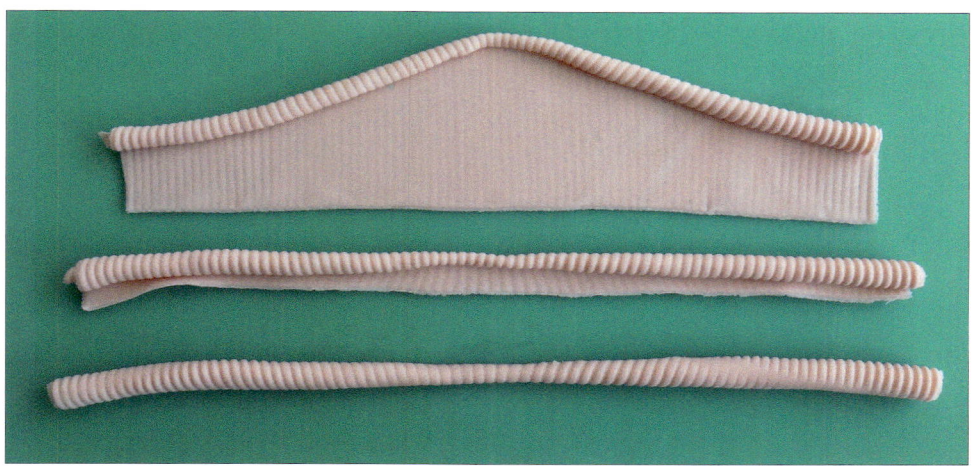

The arrangement above will create a petal or leaf that is fuller and fatter at the base or bottom and tapers at the top.

The arrangement below will create a petal or leaf that tapers at the top, is wide in the middle and tapers at the base.

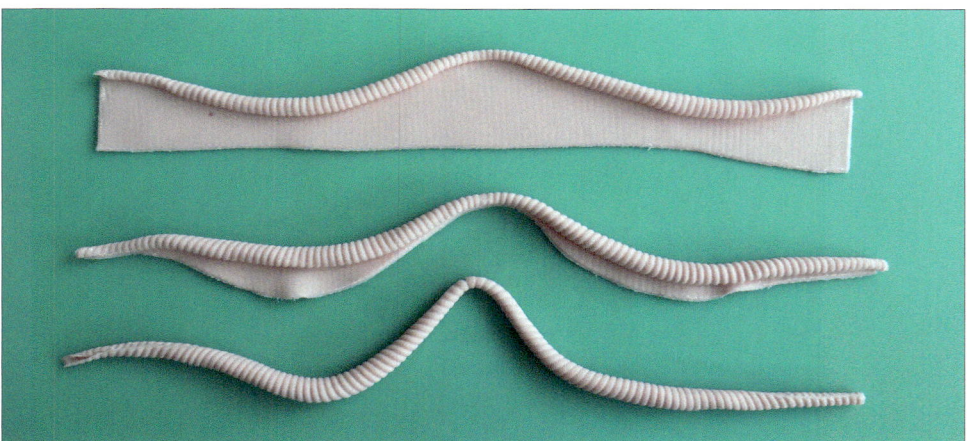

The beaded roll below has had the end sliced off to create a pointed end.

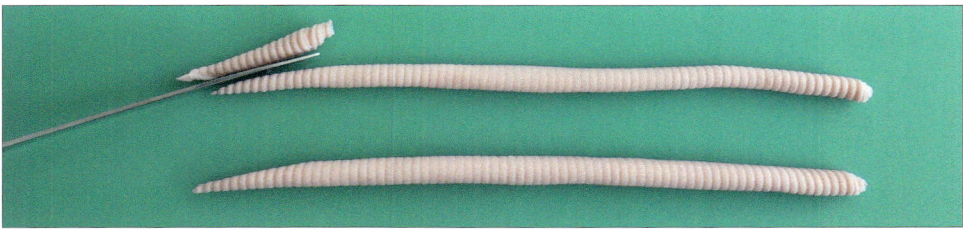

Basic Formation

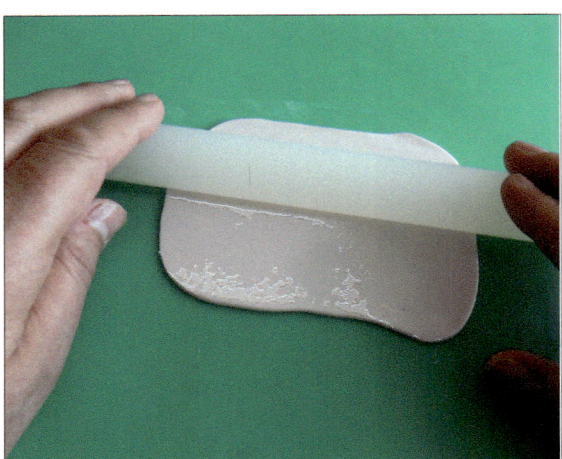

First colour your paste accordingly.

Roll out a sheet of paste or use a pasta machine. The paste should be an even thickness and on the thin side – but not too thin – if it is too thin the impression from the ribbed roller will tear.

Dust the paste sheet with icing sugar to make sure it does not stick on both sides.

The size of the sheet will depend on what size you would like the finished beaded rolls and the nature of the flower construction.

For some petals, you might need a much longer sheet of paste – for example, coiled petals - but for most standard petals you will not need a big sheet.

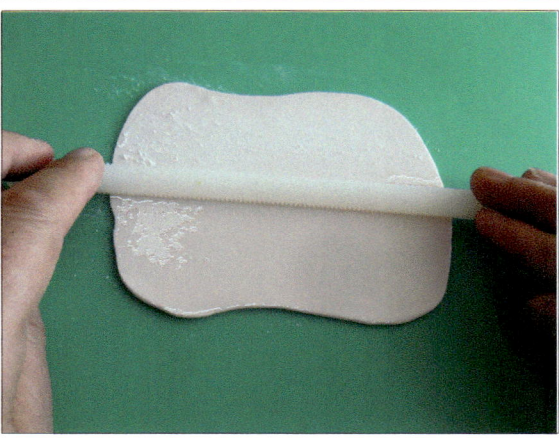

However, it is possible to create bigger sheets and then once the beaded roll is formed cut it into segments such as in half or in thirds, which saves time.

I often make a batch of the beaded rolls and store them in a sealed bag for assembly.

Before using the rollers dab more icing sugar evenly on the paste to ensure that the roller does not stick to the paste.

With the best will in the world, this can happen.

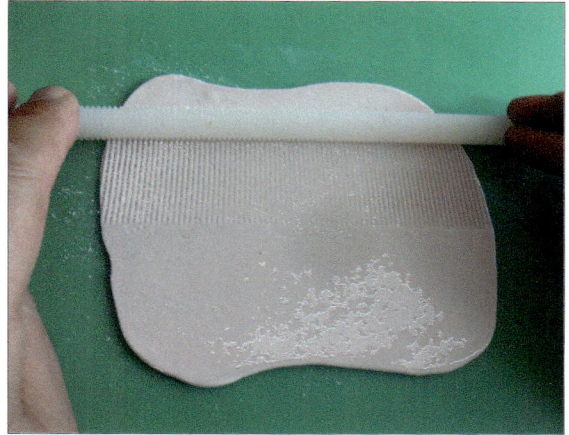

It just means you might have to start again or cut off the portion of the paste that has become distorted.

Place one of the rollers on the paste and indent the paste with the ribbed impression.

Sometimes I start at the top and work down, other times I start at the bottom and work up.

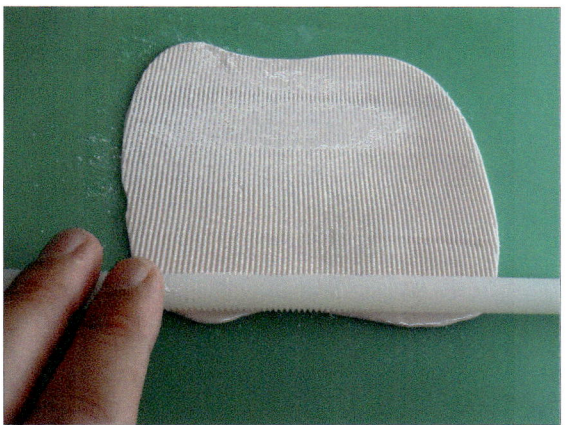

Sometimes I work from the middle and roll upward and then go back and roll down.

Once you have finished cut the sheet of paste to an even shape with straight edges.

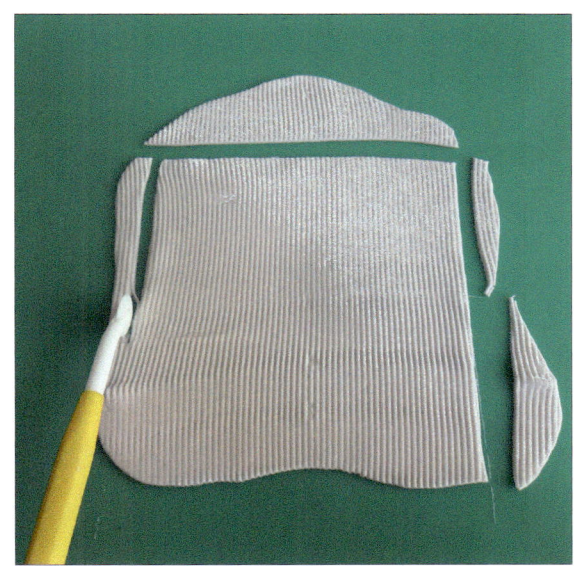

French Beaded Flowers in Sugar   17

Turn she sheet over and then start rolling the paste.

This is not an easy task to perfect and needs a little practice to master.

It is one of the basic techniques used in the creation of some of my fabric flowers that utilise a rolled edge.

Think about rolling up a sheet of paper and creating a hollow tube.

The rolled edge needs to be completely rolled up – in other words, secured with no edge showing and not merely folded.

You can lift the sheet and use both hands to create the roll along the straight edge.

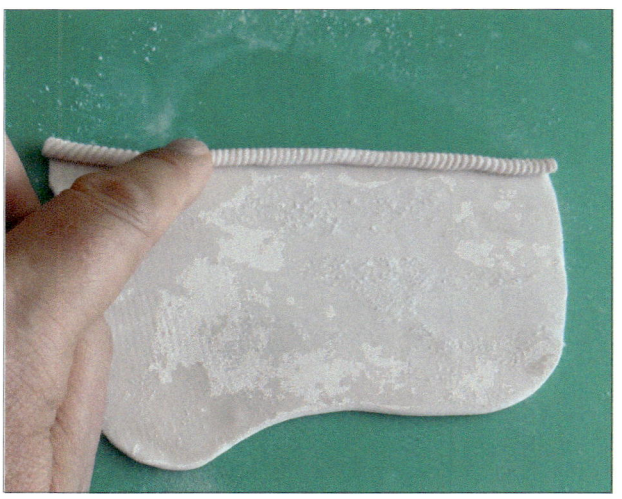

You can also roll up the edge with the sheet flat on a board by using both hands to lift the edge up a little and roll gently.

Adjustments can be made to straighten out the rolled edge and make it neater and more even by using your fingers and by the process of rolling back and forward.

Sometimes the paste can misbehave and become slightly misshapen.

Rather than start again and to combat this, I add a line of sugar glue to the edge of the paste and the developing roll to help the roll to become more secure and then continue.

This glues the roll in place and makes it easier to create a more perfect shape.

This only happens occasionally, and it is not always necessary.

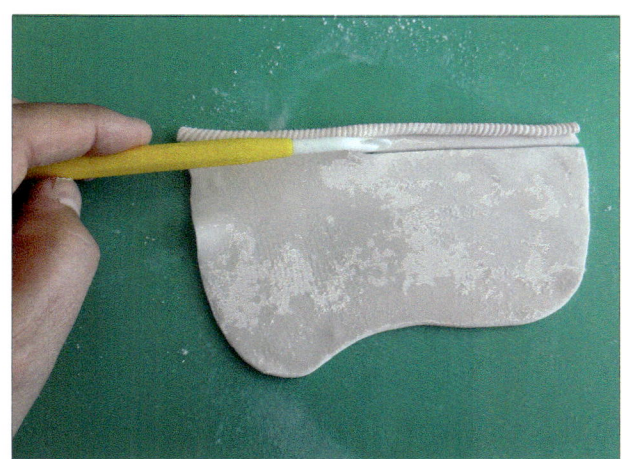

Once the first roll is tight and even, cut a straight edge with a small part of the paste remaining.

With a paintbrush add some sugar glue with a paintbrush to this exposed edge evenly and sparingly.

Then roll up the beaded roll securing the paste as you progress as best you can.

Of course, more beaded rolls can be created from the sheet of paste and stored in a sealed plastic bag.

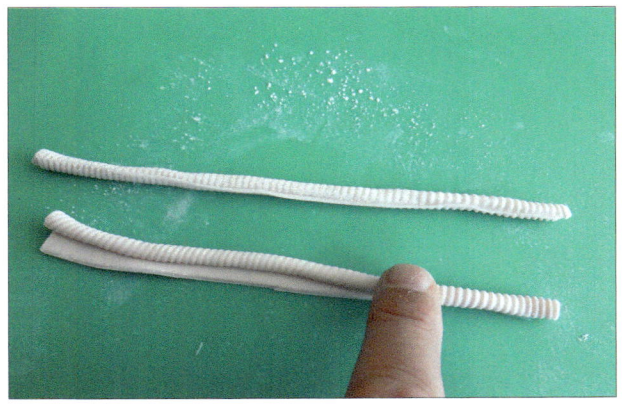

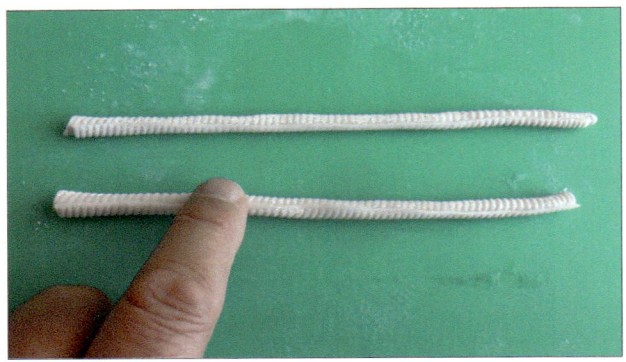

You will now have a basic beaded roll, and there will be a seam running along the roll.

Gently roll the beaded roll on the board to help secure this seam in place.

No matter what you do, this seam will rarely disappear and will always be visible. There are some cunning tricks to magically make the seam less visible by merely positioning.

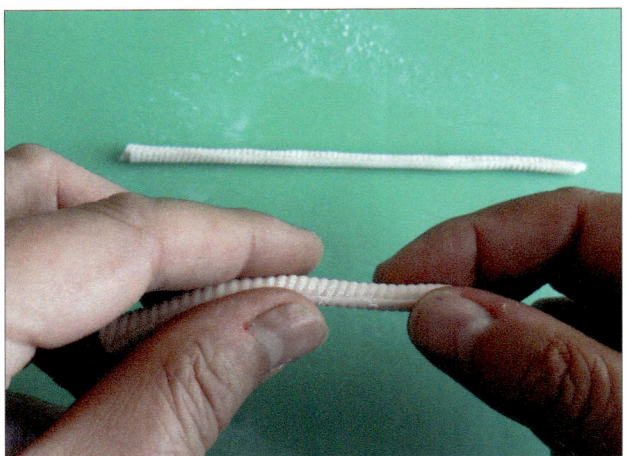

Pick up the beaded roll and with the fingers gently press the seam once again to secure.

Sometimes I leave the rolls for a few minutes in a sealed bag to settle and then repeat this process.

Next, the rolls can be formed into the basic patterns to create flower petals and the leaves.

The basic shape is a loop. As you can see in the photographs, the seam is on the underside and not visible.

Make all the loops you need and pinch and seal the ends.

Basic Formation

These individual loops can be used to form flowers as they are.

You can also add another layer to build up the formation.

Take another beaded roll and apply sugar glue to the seam along the roll and then wrap around the central loop.

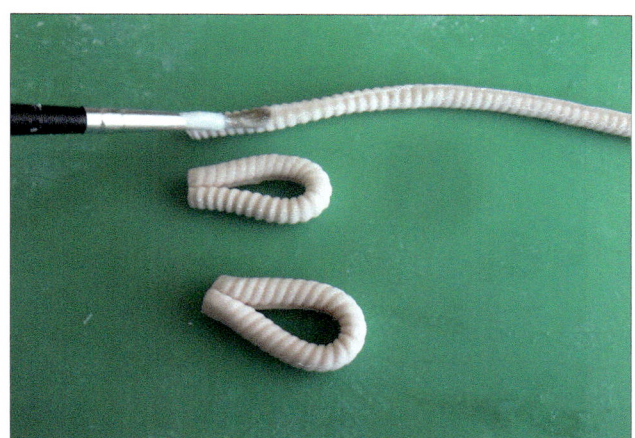

I often leave this to dry for a few minutes before I do anything with them.

Cut to shape and then pinch at the base and also make sure that the layers are stuck together. If they come apart apply more glue.

More than one layer can be created.

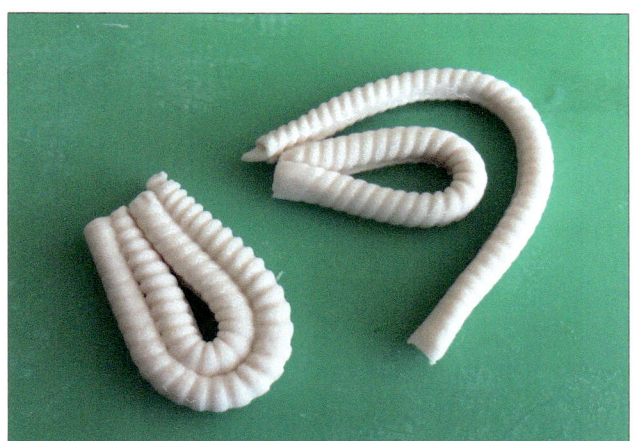

Also, an important point is that the central loop can be open or closed.

If closed, apply some sugar glue to the inside of the loop and press together.

These loops can be of various sizes from large to small and in different colours.

Wiring

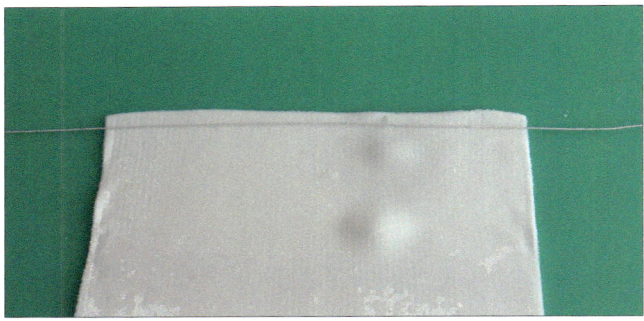

French beaded flowers in sugar can be assembled on their own without any support as seen in the first project with single looped flowers.

However, generally, they need some kind of support, so it is best to evolve the flower around a cocktail stick and a flower centre.

In some instances wiring is possible - this does ensure greater stability. This applies to both petals and leaf formations.

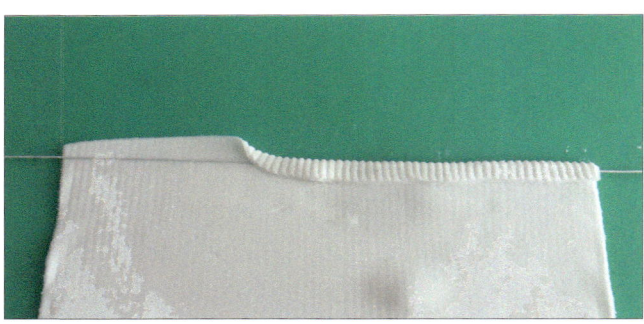

Created a ribbed sheet of paste and place a wire (usually 26 or 28g works best) at the top edge.

Add some sugar glue to the wire and the paste.

Fold the paste over and press to secure.

Add some more sugar glue.

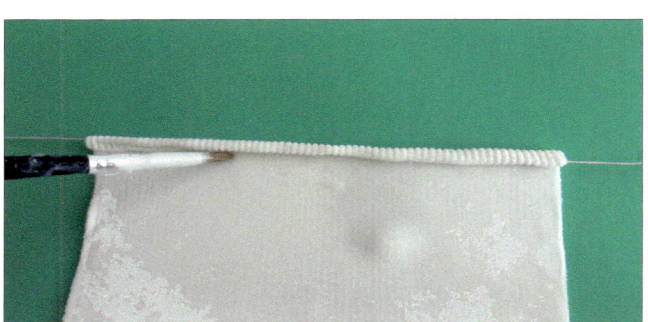

Then roll up the paste to form a beaded roll with the wire inside.

Once the first roll is tight and even, cut a straight edge with a small part of the paste remaining.

With a paintbrush add some sugar glue with a paintbrush to this exposed edge.

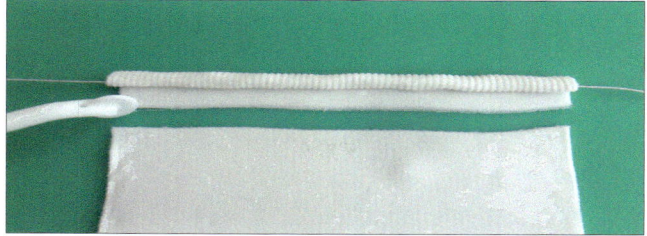

Then roll up the beaded roll securing the paste as you progress as best you can and making sure the roll is the right shape.

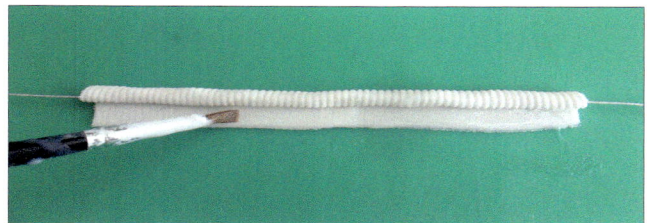

Bend the paste now to form a loop and secure the wire at the base with floral tape.

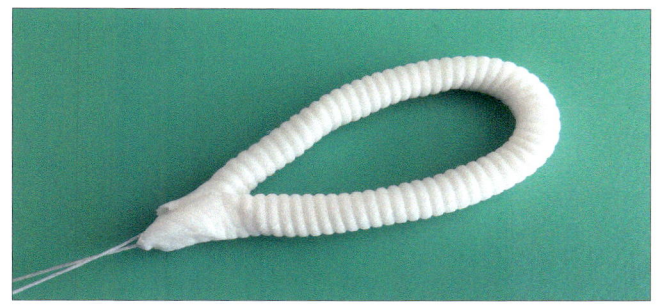

Wiring works particular well with leaf formations. In this instance, there is only need for one central wired piece. All other loops can be glued alongside.

Leaves

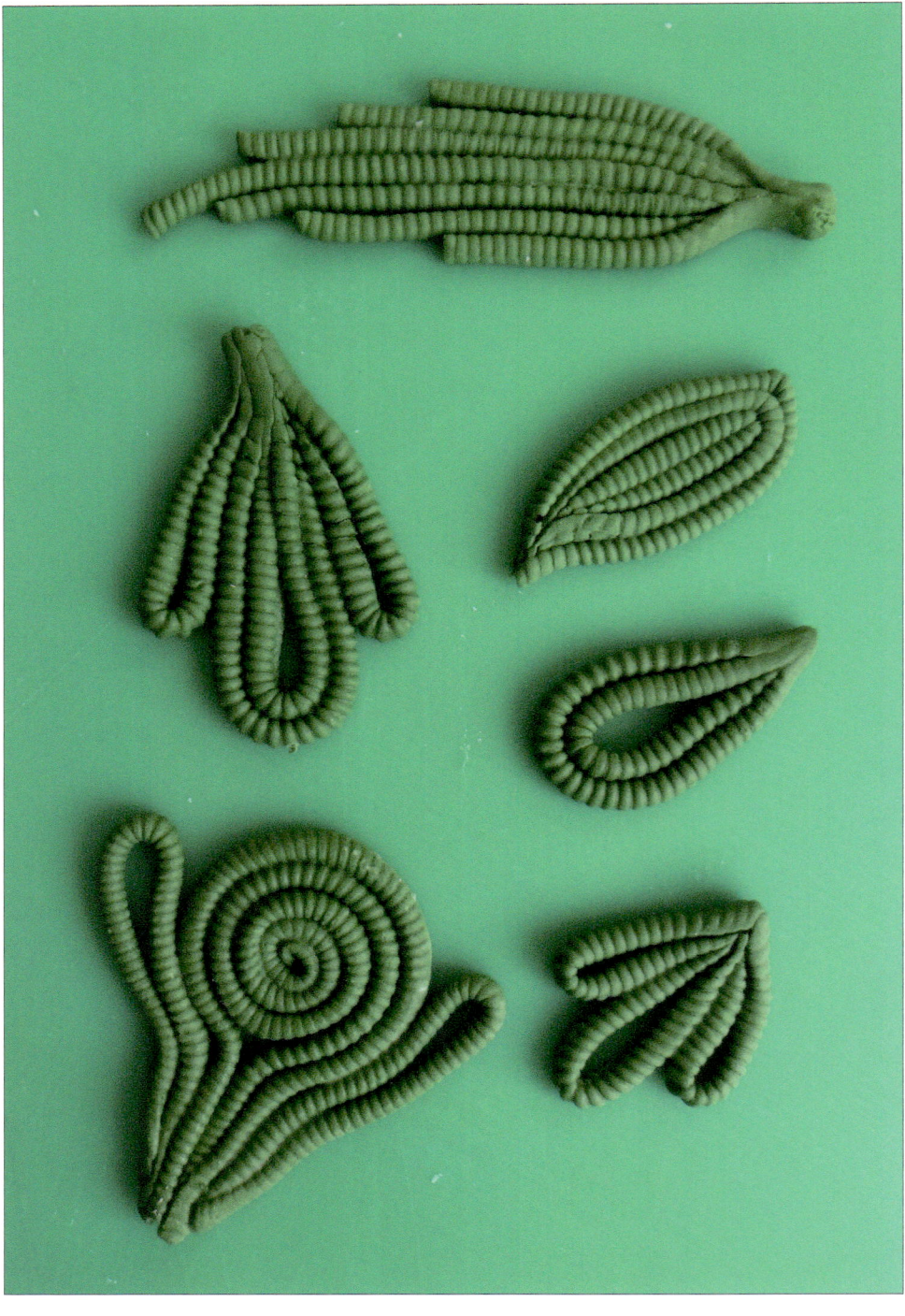

Leaf construction follows the same principles and formation as petals with the addition of perhaps a few more twists, such as my application of pointed ends.

Simple, Single-Looped French Beaded Flowers

Simple, single-looped flowers are the easiest and most straightforward expression of French beaded flowers in sugar.

The arrangement of petals is created using three, four, or six single loops with an accompanying simple leaf arrangement made of two loops.

The cake used for the flowers is a single creation made to resemble a gift box and an ideal birthday or celebration cake.

The cake is painted with a unique paint effect of a light orange-cream base wash and an appliqued darker orange-brown layer that is meant to replicate crushed or brushed velvet.

The border is created using an ornate braiding mould that will be available via Nicholas Lodge and Katy Sue Designs. A similar alternative can be used such as the Plaited Borders mould from Karen Davies.

Simple, Single-Looped French Beaded Flower

French Beaded Flowers in Sugar

From a base beaded roll, create a variety of loops to form the petals of the looped flowers.

There are small flowers of three loops and four loops and large flowers comprising six loops and some large six looped flowers with an inner layer of four loops.

For the smaller flowers of three and four loops attach to each other one by one with some glue, upside down, pinch the end, cut off any excess and place in a former.

For the larger flowers, seal the loops at the base and then arrange in a former and glue together with sugar glue. Allow to dry completely.

Once dried, attach a small round ball of yellow paste with glue in the middle of the flower and indent the centre with a cocktail stick.

For the smaller leaves, make two simple loops in green paste one bigger than the other with the seam on the underside and attach with glue.

I placed one set on each side of the small looped flowers.

For the larger leaves create one inner loop, then glue the underside of another piece of a beaded roll and wrap around the central loop.

Pinch the base together and adjust and store in a sealed plastic bag until required.

Glue the underside of the dried flowers and attach the leaves while still soft and not dried out. Turn and place in formers to dry and adjust to suit adding pieces of kitchen roll underneath each leaf to give form and shape. Once dry glue to the cake.

More Elaborate, Single-Looped French Beaded Flower

Still using the premise of simple, single-loops, this French beaded flower is more ambitious with a base centre on a cocktail stick.

One flower has one layer, and the two larger flowers have two layers. For the larger flowers, there is an inner layer of six petals and an outer layer of eight petals with an accompanying leaf arrangement made of several loops around a central wired loop.

The cake used for the flowers is a two-tier creation that would make an ideal birthday or celebration cake and could also be expanded into a wedding cake with a third tier.

The cake is painted with a unique paint effect of a light orange base wash and an appliqued, stippled off-white top layer.

The border is created using a pearl mould from Karen Davies Cakes and part of the Debonair mould from Marvelous Moulds.

French Beaded Flowers in Sugar

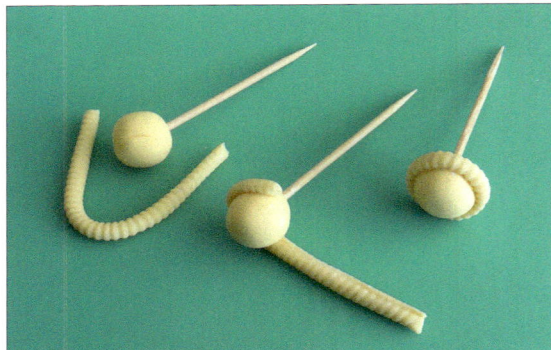

First, create the central flower centre. Make a small pea sized ball of yellow paste and glue to a cocktail stick and allow to dry completely.

Next, make a tight, small beaded roll in the same coloured paste.

Add glue to the side of the yellow ball and carefully attach the beaded roll with the seam underneath.

Snip the end to complete the circle of beads on the ball. Allow to dry again.

Create the six loops for the inner petals and glue to the underside of the flower centre. Place in a former and allow to dry.

Next, create the eight larger loops for the outer petals. Turn the flower with the centre and six inner petals upside down and glue each of the eight petals in turn onto the back of the flower.

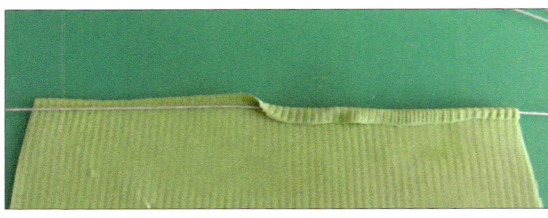

Place in a former and allow to dry.

Next make the leaves. For the wired central part of the leaf, roll out a sheet of green paste that has been indented with the ribbed roller.

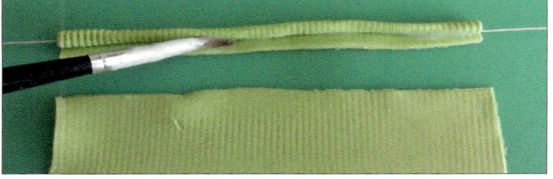

Place a wire (usually 26 or 28g works best) at the top edge.

Add some sugar glue to the wire and the paste. Fold the paste over and press to secure and add some more sugar glue.

Then roll up the paste with the wire inside. Adjust and cut a straight edge with a small part of the paste remaining.

With a paintbrush add more sugar glue to this exposed edge. Then roll up securing the paste as you progress and making sure the roll is the right shape.

Bend the paste now to form a loop and secure with tape.

I have used three leaves per flower. The largest leaf has four more unwired loops - two larger and two smaller. The smaller just two.

For each, paint glue on one side of each loop and attach on either side of the central loop (also with glue on each side).

Leave for a few minutes and then pinch together at the base.

Angle and shape and leave to dry on foam to suit the floral arrangement.

Once dry attach to the flower with floral tape.

Single and Double-Looped French Beaded Flower

Still using the premise of simple, single-loops, this French beaded flower has a base centre on a cocktail stick with the addition of double loops on the largest flower.

One flower has one layer of ten single loops, the medium sized flower has two layers of single loops, and the largest flower has three layers – two layers of single loops and an outer double-looped layer.

There is an accompanying leaf arrangement made of several loops around a central wired beaded roll.

The cake used for the flowers is a two-tier creation that would make an ideal birthday or celebration cake and could also be expanded into a wedding cake with a third tier.

The cake is painted with a unique paint effect of a light mauve base wash and an appliqued, bagged, darker, mauve-purple top layer.

The border is created using a pearl mould from Karen Davies Cakes.

French Beaded Flowers in Sugar 37

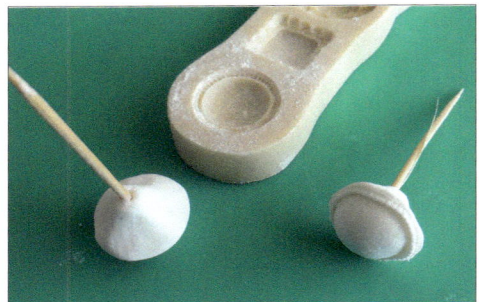

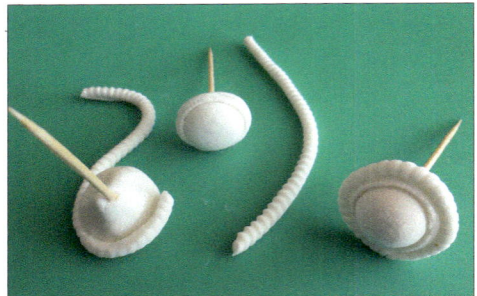

First, create the central flower centre. Make a small sized ball of white paste and insert into a jewellery mould. Insert a glued cocktail stick into this shape and secure the paste. Dry completely.

Next, make a tight, small beaded roll in the white paste but use the largest ribbed roller to create the largest beads.

Add glue to the side of the jewelled centre and carefully attach the beaded roll with the seam underneath.

Snip the end to complete the circle of beads on the ball. Allow to dry again.

Create the loops for the inner petals and glue to the underside of the flower centre. Place in a former and allow to dry.

Gradually build up the other layers of petalled loops.

For the double loops refer back to the creation of the leaves in the first project and follow the instructions.

Single and Double-Looped French Beaded Flower

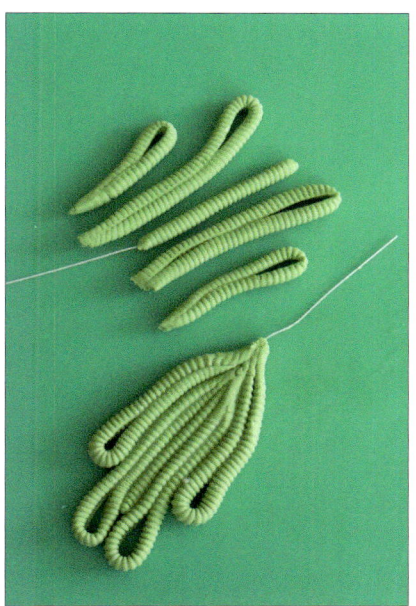

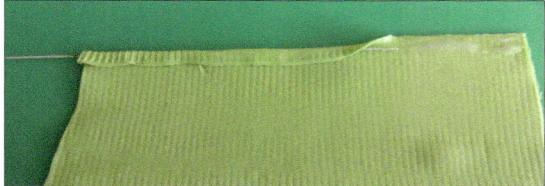

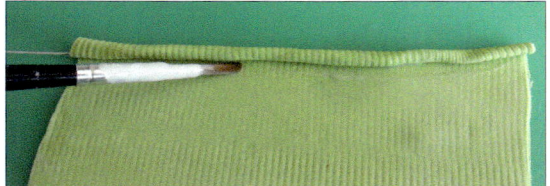

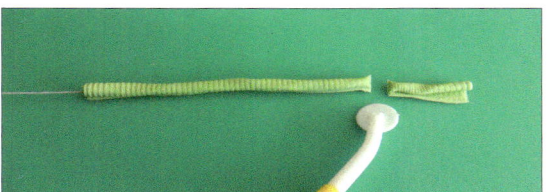

To create the leaves follow the principles in the previous project and follow the photograph on the right.

In this instance, the central part of the leaf is a single, wired, beaded roll. The end is cut neatly and rounded.

Glue the single loops either side.

For the larger leaf, there are three rows of single loops on either side.

Once formed and dried attach to the flower with floral tape.

Single-Looped, Cluster French Beaded Flower

Using simple, single-loops, this French beaded flower comprises an arrangement of multiple loops to form what is called a cluster.

There are two sizes of flower. Both begin with two loops glued on a cocktail stick. The smaller arrangement then has one layer of six looped petals, and the larger flower has three layers of four looped petals increasing in size slightly to the outer layer. A far more elaborate and grand flower is shown above on the left.

There are two accompanying leaf arrangements. The first comprises three simple loops and the second a coiled leaf.

The cake used for the flowers is a two-tier creation with a third base, that would make an ideal birthday or celebration cake and could also be expanded into a wedding cake with another tier.

The cake is painted with a unique and subtle paint effect of light grey sponging.

The base tier is covered in a ribbed silver wrap, edged with an embossed pink bow and fabric band and a matching band on the top tier.

French Beaded Flowers in Sugar

First, create a group of simple loops with a purple colouring. Size will depend on the cake and the tier you will be using for the flowers.

Glue the base of two loops and lay a cocktail stick on one and then add the second on top and squeeze together and secure.

Leave to dry with a gap between them (add a rolled up piece of kitchen roll).

I often dry these upside down inserted into a piece of green flower oasis.

When dry, glue the other looped petals to the centre of the two loops and leave to dry in a former with support from rolled up pieces of kitchen roll to give shape.

For the larger flowers repeat this process allowing the various stages to dry completely before adding each layer.

The first leaf arrangement on the middle tier comprises three simple loops.

Single-Looped, Cluster French Beaded Flower 42

Make the loops in green paste - one larger loops and two smaller. Add glue to each side of the large loop and one side of the smaller loops and glue together. Leave to dry for a few minutes and then pinch and seal.

The second left arrangement is formed of a simple coil. Here you will need to create a longer beaded roll.

Cut the end to form a point, add glue along one side and simple roll up to form the coil.

These leaves can be glued to the cake and the flowers added and glued or glued and attached to the cluster flower and left in a former to dry before being inserted in the cake.

Coiled, Spiral French Beaded Flower

A stylised, almost art deco fantasy flower, created using coiled beaded rolls to form four petals arranged around an ornate jewelled centre.

The addition of a flared leaf arrangement of three leaves per flower adds to the dramatic flair.

The cake used for the flowers is a two-tier creation with a third base, that would make an ideal birthday or celebration cake and could also be expanded into a wedding cake with third tier.

The cake is painted with a unique paint effect of a pink base wash and appliqued silver decoration.

The border is created using an ornate art deco mould, painted grey to match the paint effects from Pilar Gonzalez Nugent at Sunflower Sugar Art.

French Beaded Flowers in Sugar

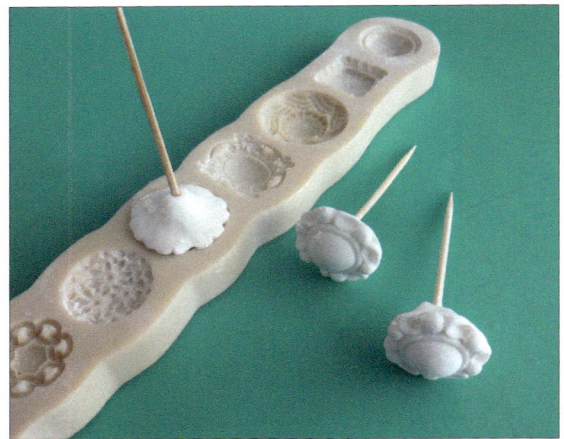

First, create the central flower centre. Take a small sized ball of white paste and insert into a jewellery mould.

Insert a glued cocktail stick into this shape and secure the paste. Dry completely.

Once dry, paint silver (it needs to be painted rather than dusted as the effect will be more vibrant - use silver powder and clear alcohol) and once again allow to dry.

For each coiled petal use deep red paste. You will need a very long sheet of paste to create a very long beaded roll to form each of the four petals.

I use a big sheet and create four beaded rolls and store them in a sealed plastic bag until required.

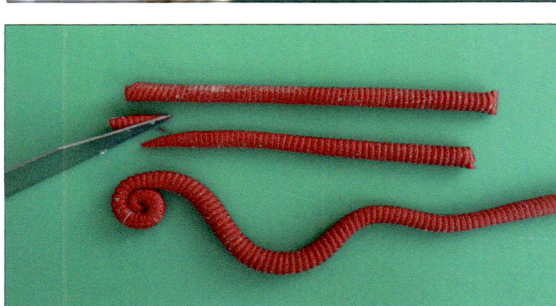

Cut the end of the beaded roll to form a point, add glue along one side (usually the seam) and roll up to form the coil.

Leave to dry for a few minutes and squeeze together slightly. You may need to add some more glue if the roll has not stuck together well enough. This is best done by reversing the petal and adding the glue on the reverse side.

Another tip is to dab the petals with icing sugar back and front to stop them sticking to the surface as they dry.

Another consideration is how to disguise the seam.

When you evolve the petals try and secure the seam against the side of the roll, so you wind it up, glue it and conceal it.

Once you have the four petals, press one end of each petal to form a very slight V shape.

Add glue to the top side of each V and arrange each petal in a neat overlapping formation in a former.

It is also useful to spray cake release onto the former, which will help prevent the flower from sticking to the former.

Take the silver painted jewelled centre and apply glue to the base and insert into the centre with tweezers and press down to secure in the centre of the petals.

Carefully lift up each petal and add pieces of kitchen roll to give support and give the flower a neat concave shape.

Leave to dry in a former.

It is possible to leave for a few hours and then turn upside down and remove the flower from the former and gently press the base to ensure the centre is stuck to the petals. Place back into the former and dry further.

French Beaded Flowers in Sugar

For larger petals, you will need a very long beaded roll, but it is possible to use two pieces and stick together.

Make two long pieces of a beaded roll. Create the core petal as detailed above and when you come to the end of the roll, cut the end to form a point.

Cut the end of the second beaded roll to form another point and glue the base (as usual) and attach to the first and central coiled beaded roll.

Although you might see some part of the join between the two points of the beaded roll, it will enable you to make a larger petal and will not be too noticeable.

At the same time, for the outer edges of the coiled petal, and this second piece you might want to increase the size of the beaded roll and make the roll increase in size toward the end.

Make sure you secure well with glue and dust the base to stop the petal sticking.

For the flared leaves make four pieces of a beaded roll in green paste.

Cut to shape with each piece having a point and each piece lining up to be large through to smaller.

Glue all four pieces together and seal and secure the base.

Arrange and shape the leaf into a flared arrangement and allow to dry for a while.

Turn the dried, coiled flower upside down and add glue to the base of the flower and the leaves and then attach the leaves.

Place the flower and the leaves in a former and add pieces of kitchen roll underneath the leaves to add shape and allow to dry.

Daisy
French Beaded Flower

The Daisy uses interlinking and overlapping loops as petals that are arranged around a delicate coiled centre.

The leaf arrangement comprises single and double loops.

The cake used for the flowers is a two-tier creation that would make an ideal birthday or celebration cake and could also be expanded into a wedding cake with third tier.

The cake is painted with a unique paint effect of brushed and sponged panels with an appliqued gold decoration.

The white border is created using an ornate deco floral mould. A similar alternative can be used such as the Plaited Borders mould from Karen Davies.

Make the flower centres first of all. Take a ball of yellow paste and on a work surface flatten one side and create a cone. Insert a glued cocktail stick into the cone and allow to dry completely.

With the same yellow paste make a thin beaded roll and cut the end to form a point. Glue the base and wind up to form a simple coil (as seen in the previous project with the construction of the petals for the coiled petals).

Glue the top of the flattened cone and attach the coil. The coil should be slightly bigger than the flat cone so that it covers it completely.

Secure and allow to dry.

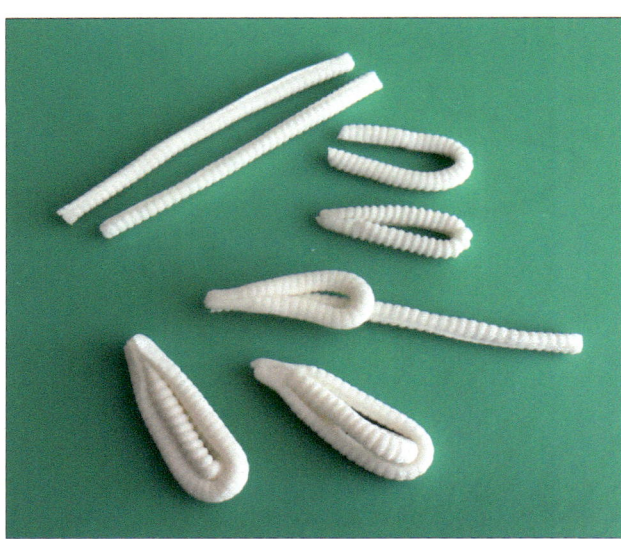

For the individual petals create many strips of white beaded rolls. Each petal comprises two loops one large than the other. Wrap the second, larger loop around the first loop.

Squeeze the base and pinch and seal.

It is best to create all the petals for each flower first and store in a sealed plastic bag before assembly.

On this particular cake, the smaller and medium flowers have ten petals and the largest flower twelve petals. Each petal loop for each flower is a different length ranging from smaller to larger.

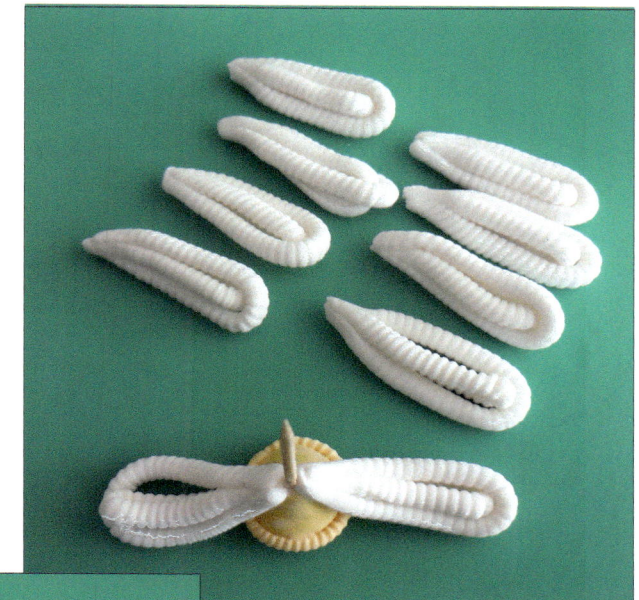

Attach the looped petals one by one and build up the arrangement. Press each petal firmly to ensure they adhere to the centre.

Each petal has to be shaped to become narrow at the base to fit the centre.

Turn the flower centre upside down and add glue to the base and glue the petal loops to the centre.

Place a former over the flower and then invert to the right side up and place in a former.

Adjust all the petals with a paintbrush if necessary to ensure they are all in the right position.

Add pieces of kitchen roll underneath the petal loops to add shape and allow to dry.

It is possible to leave for a few hours and then turn upside down and remove the flower from the former and gently press the base to ensure the centre is stuck to the petals. Place back into the former and dry further.

Daisy French Beaded Flower

For the leaves use green paste. Create a central double loop and attach single loops on either side.

Allow to dry and settle for a while. Then turn the flower upside down and add glue and attach the leaves.

Place the flower and the leaves in a former and add pieces of kitchen roll underneath the leaves to add shape and allow to dry.

The large flower and leaves may not fit a former- this is not a problem – simply dry upside down on a flat card surface cushioned with kitchen roll.

Blossom
French Beaded Flower

The blossom is an arrangement of three triple loops with a further three triple backing loops making a six-looped flower, all around an ornate jewelled centre with a double looped edge.

The pointed leaves are formed of multiple loops.

The cake used for the flowers is a three-tier creation that would make an ideal birthday or celebration cake and could also be expanded in size into a wedding cake.

The cake is painted with a unique paint effect to resemble delicate marbling.

The white border is created using an ornate braiding mould that will be available via Nicholas Lodge and Katy Sue Designs. A similar alternative can be used such as the Plaited Borders mould from Karen Davies.

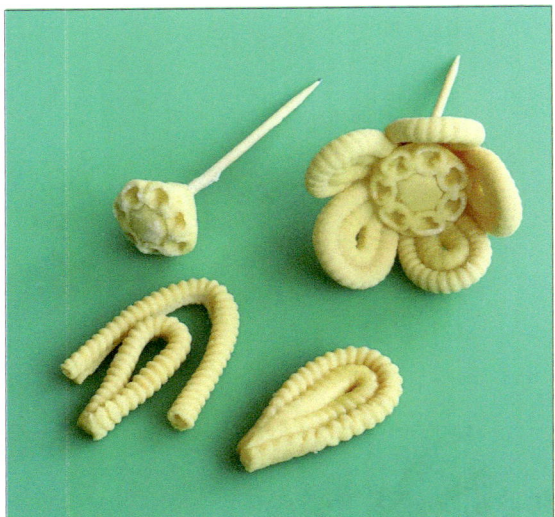

First, create the central flower centre. Make a small sized ball of yellow paste and insert into a jewellery mould.

Insert a glued cocktail stick into this shape and secure the paste. Dry completely.

Create five small double loops in yellow paste and glue to the base of the jewelled centre and allow to dry completely.

Next, create the six multi-looped petals in a salmon pink paste. These petals are quite long, and you require three sizes for each of the flowers on the cake – small, medium and large.

The petals are each formed of three loops.

Attach the first three looped petals to the underside of the jewelled centre with glue and allow to dry in a former. These petals are more convex in shape and are supported underneath with small pieces of kitchen roll.

When dry, add the other three looped petals and repeat the drying and shaping process.

On this cake, two buds are placed on either side of each flower.

These are created with a small double looped petal in salmon pink around the central jewelled centre.

The two leaves either side of the flowers are a simple arrangement of multiple loops in green paste. Once created glue to the reverse of the flower, shape and allow to dry.

Fantasy, Multi-Coloured, Blossom French Beaded Flower

This fantasy blossom flower introduces a twist with two adjoining central loops and the idea of creating the petals in multi-coloured loops.

The centre of the flower petals – the two adjacent central loops – are surrounded by three layers of beaded rolls in complementary shading, and there is a multi-looped green centre.

The leaves are formed of a coil and overlying loops and are also multi-coloured.

The cake used for the flowers is a two-tier creation that would make an ideal birthday or celebration cake and could also be expanded into a wedding cake with third tier.

The cake is painted with a unique paint effect of very gentle sponging.

The border is created using a braiding mould and a pearl edge in white. The braiding mould will be available via Nicholas Lodge and Katy Sue Designs. A similar alternative can be used such as the Plaited Borders mould from Karen Davies.

French Beaded Flowers in Sugar

First create a group of small, simple loops in green paste.

Follow the same principle as the beginning central part of the cluster flower project.

Glue the base of two loops and lay a cocktail stick on one and then add the second on top and squeeze together and secure.

Leave to dry with a gap between them (add a rolled up piece of kitchen roll.)

I often dry these upside down inserted into a piece of green flower oasis.

When dry, glue the other looped petals to the centre of the two loops and leave to dry in a former with support from rolled up pieces of kitchen roll to give shape.

I have made small, medium and large centres with six loops for the small centre, eleven for the medium and fifteen for the large centre.

There is no rhyme or reason here it was just to do with what looked best for each flower size.

Each flower is made with four petals and from four different coloured pastes – ranging from light cream to darker cream and a creamy-orange.

To make each petal, first, create the central part of two adjoining central loops.

There are three flower sizes - small, medium and large. It is best to try and measure the beaded roll for the central part of each flower to ensure consistency.

Make a beaded roll in light cream and form two loops. Glue both loops together almost to form a heart shape and squeeze and secure the end.

Allow to dry for a short while and ensure the two loops are glued and stable.

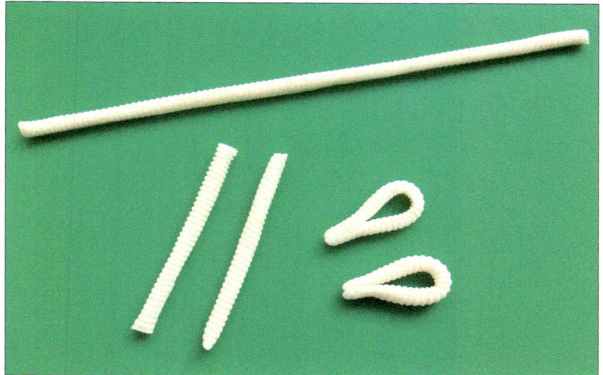

Then create the other beaded rolls in the various shades and wrap one by one around the central loops, making sure they are glued securely.

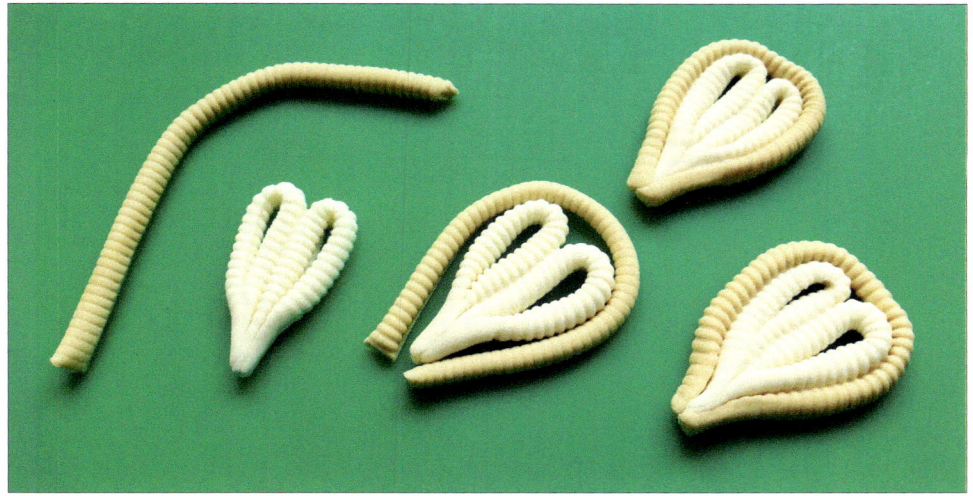

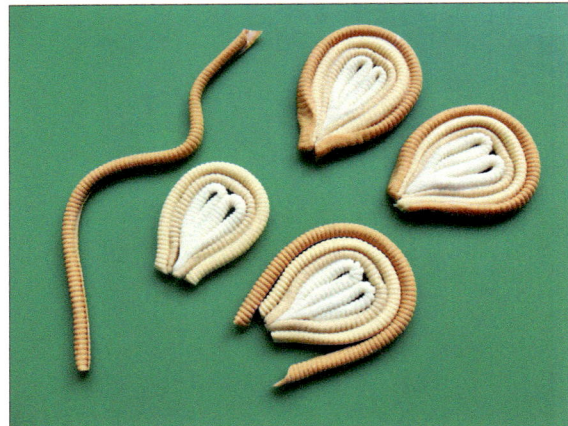

It is also wise to increase the size of the rolls as you progress outward – so that the last creamy-orange roll is thicker than the others.

Squeeze the ends and secure making sure everything is stable, tight and glued properly.

It is best to make the petals of the flowers in batches – in other words, create four petals for each flower and assemble then move onto the next flower and another four petals.

When the four petals are complete, dust the base with icing sugar and leave to settle for maybe 20-30 minutes turning them once or twice to dry a little.

Then cut off the pointed ends, add some glue to the base and arrange in an overlapping fashion in a former, pressing gently in the middle to secure and stick the petals together without damaging any of the impressions on the rolls.

Take the centre of the small green loops and apply glue to the base and add some more glue in the middle of the flower and insert into the flower using tweezers. Adjust accordingly.

It is possible to leave for a few hours and then turn upside down and remove the flower from the former and very carefully and gently press the base to ensure the centre is stuck to the petals.

Place back into the former and dry further.

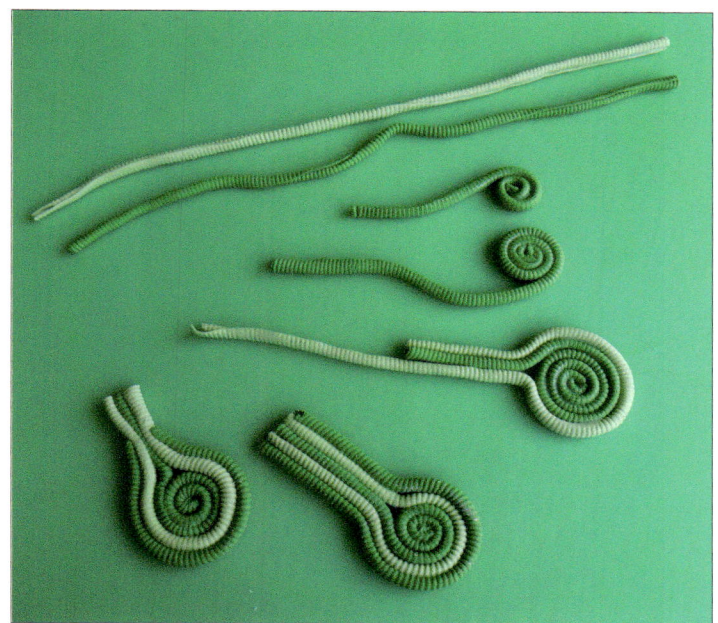

The leaves comprise two shades of green – one dark, the other lighter. The base is a coil – described in earlier projects like the coiled, spiral flower and one of the leaves in the cluster flower project.

Once you have made the coil, in a darker green paste, leave the end as a base to attach other layers.

Wrap and glue a lighter green roll around the central coil and then add and glue another darker green beaded roll. Then cut and shape.

Leave for a short while to settle and then glue to the underside of the flower.

Each flower has three leaves. The size of each leaf can vary by making the central coil smaller or bigger. Also, extra rolled layers can be applied.

Gardenia or Magnolia French Beaded Flower

This stylish arrangement could form either a gardenia or magnolia and is composed of simple white looped petals constructed around a coiled beaded centre.

There are no leaves as such but a simple pointed green beaded roll as a tendril from either side with the addition of side buds.

The cake used for the flowers is a two-tier creation that would make an ideal birthday or celebration cake and could also be expanded into a wedding cake with third tier.

The cake is painted with a unique paint effect of a base coat of light green with overlying variegated marbling and brush painting.

The white border is created using a lily lace mould from Pilar Gonzalez Nugent at Sunflower Sugar Art.

French Beaded Flowers in Sugar

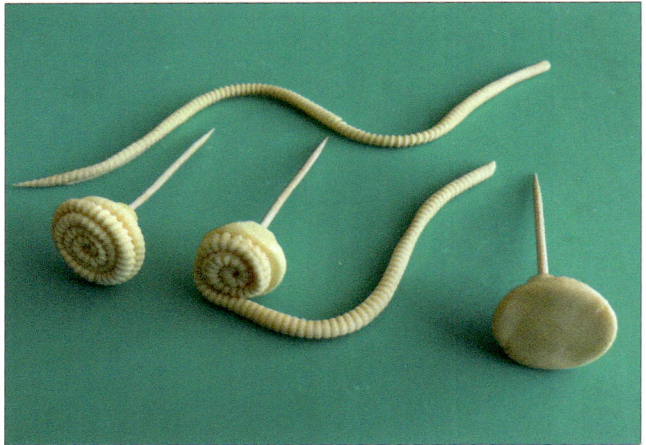

Make the flower centres first of all and follow the instructions given at the beginning of the Daisy project.

Take a ball of yellow paste and flatten one side. Insert a glued cocktail stick and allow to dry completely. Make a thin yellow beaded roll and cut the end to form a point and create asimple coil. Glue to the flattened cone, secure and allow to dry.

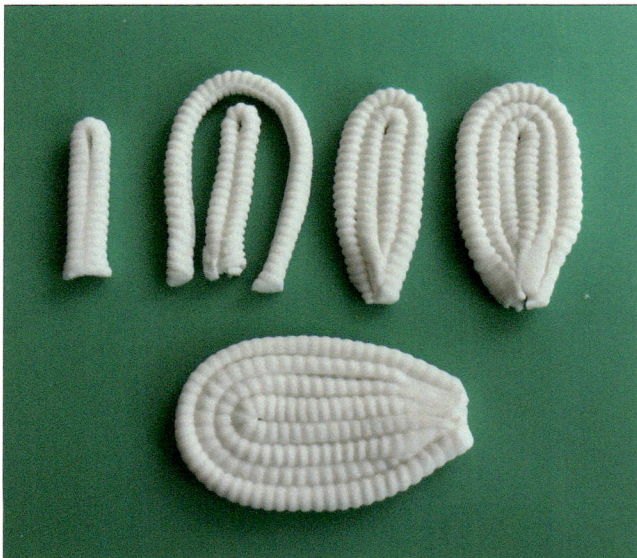

Next, make the petals in an arrangement of three. Each set of petals varies in size and has differing numbers of white beaded rolls (the photographs show four).

For the smaller flower the inner layer has two, for the medium flower there are three, and the large flower has four. The second layer of petals is the same as the inner layer. The third and fourth layers have three rolls on the smaller flower, for the medium flower, the third layer has three rolls and the fourth four rolls, and for the larger flower, the third and fourth layers have four rolls.

For the centre, which also forms the buds, attach the three petals with glue to the underside of the yellow coiled centre and shape the petals to fold inward.

I often dry these upside down inserted into a piece of green flower oasis or in a former right side up.

Create more petals and attach in layers of three to the centre.

Dry each set before attaching further sets of three.

Adjust accordingly and support the petals underneath with small pieces of kitchen roll.

Blue, Fantasy French Beaded Flower

This blue fantasy arrangement has multi-coloured looped petals in shades of blue in a similar construction to the earlier multi-coloured fantasy flower but with the addition of a centre made with vertical beaded rolls.

The leaves are formed of a coil with overlying loops and side loops.

The cake used for the flowers is a two-tier creation that would make an ideal birthday or celebration cake and could also be expanded into a wedding cake with third tier.

The cake is painted with a unique paint effect of dappling also called frottage or fratting.

The white border is created using an impression mould that produces a fabric band with a pearl edge. An alternative can be used such as the Plaited Borders mould from Karen Davies.

French Beaded Flowers in Sugar

First, make the flower centres. Insert a glued cocktail stick into a cone-shaped piece of paste and allow to dry.

Create thin, pale yellow beaded rolls and cut into small pieces to fit the side of the cone.

Cut one end to form a point.

Add glue to the cone and affix all the pointed pieces.

It is best to start by adding four pieces like dividing a circle into four and then adding the other pieces into the gaps.

Ensure all pieces fit perfectly and flatten to the underside of the cone.

Allow to dry completely.

Next, create eight small loops in a slighter darker yellow paste in three sized lengths – small, medium and large and glue to each of the flower centres. **Dry completely.**

Blue, Fantasy French Beaded Flower

The petals are made out of two shades of blue paste – one darker the other lighter – and white. The arrangement is in two sets of three and comprise small, medium and large lengths to create the three different sizes of flowers.

Create all the petals for each flower in batches of three. Attach the first three petals to the centre with glue upside down and then invert and place in a former. Adjust accordingly and support the petals underneath with small pieces of kitchen roll. Allow to dry before adding the final three petals.

The small flower has one loop or beaded roll of dark blue as the centre of the petal. The other two petals have double loops for the centre. All the flowers have a further two beaded rolls surrounding the centre in light blue and large beaded roll in white surrounding all of them.

French Beaded Flowers in Sugar

The leaves are created in green paste and follow the same principle seen in the fantasy, multi-coloured flower project. The base is a coil with the end as a base to attach other layers.

Wrap and glue another green roll around the central coil and then glue further loops either side. Leave for a short while to settle and then glue to the underside of the flower and dry completely.

Rose
French Beaded Flower

The arrangement of looped petals in various shades of cream works well to emulate a typical authentic French beaded rose and is complemented by pointed green looped leaves.

The cake used for the flowers is a three-tier creation that would make an ideal celebration or wedding cake. There is a small but deep top tier, the middle tier comprises three cakes the same size as the top tier and rests on a shallow third tier.

The cake is painted with a base layer of light lavender paint with additional single line brushstrokes and is smoothed over with a light brushing of off-white lustre dust using a soft pad.

The cream border on the top two tiers is created from a small art deco mould from Pilar Gonzalez Nugent at Sunflower Sugar Art, complemented with pearl edging and an additional weaved moulded design on the bottom tier.

The top of the cake features a dramatic twisted fabric flourish in cream to match the overall colour scheme.

Rose French Beaded Flower

A perennial favourite for many craft decorations – the rose – is not so simple to replicate in sugar as a French beaded flower, primarily because it is not an easy task to shape the petals to overlap and interlink without them losing their integrity.

However, this flower is reasonable easy to assemble without the overlapping and on this cake, there are two sizes.

For the smaller rose, first create two small, double loops or petals in a darker cream paste and one triple loop.

Follow the same principle as the beginning central part of the cluster flower project, but in this instance, the petal is formed of three pieces of beaded roll glued together.

Glue the base of the two double looped petals and lay a cocktail stick on one and then add the second on top and squeeze together and secure.

Then glue the third triple looped petal in place covering one of the gaps between the two smaller petals.

Leave to dry with gaps between the petals (add a rolled up piece of kitchen roll). I often dry these upside down inserted into a piece of green flower oasis or in a former right side up.

Next, create three more triple petalled loops in a lighter shade of cream and then affix to the existing centre. Leave to dry in a former and shape accordingly.

Create another three petals in an even lighter shade of cream, but with four loops and glue to the existing flower. Leave to dry in a former and shape.

French Beaded Flowers in Sugar

Surrounding these five petals as the core, are a further five petals of a lighter shade of cream made up of four loops.

Glue these to the central group and allow to dry.

This is best done upside down.

For the large flowers, the centre is made up of two double lopped petals. Make these first (as above) and allow to dry completely.

These are then surrounded by a group of three triple looped petals arrange at angles.

Next, make another five large petals in a light cream comprising four loops of beaded rolls and slightly large in size.

Glue these again to the central flower and place in a former to dry and shape accordingly, supporting the petals underneath with small pieces of kitchen roll.

Each rose has four leaves. For the smaller rose, these are made up of three beaded rolls, and the large leaves are made of four beaded rolls.

Gently pinch the end of each leaf to form a point. Glue and affix to the back of the flower. Leave to dry in a former or upside down.

Poppy
French Beaded Flower

A dramatic and colourful French beaded flower, the Poppy is a more adventurous flower to make being formed with a yellow looped centre with black looped surround and then two layers of four red petals.

This flower is complemented by an arrangement of three green leaves created with central loops and pointed single beaded rolls on either side.

The cake used for the flowers is a two-tier creation that would make an ideal celebration or wedding cake.

The cake is painted with a paint effect that comprises applying a base layer of mid-cream and then removing with a spatula.

The border is created using an ornate braiding mould that will be available via Nicholas Lodge and Katy Sue Designs. A similar alternative can be used such as the Plaited Borders mould from Karen Davies.

First, make the centre. Create four small, yellow loops and follow the same principle as the beginning central part of the cluster flower project.

Glue the base of the two loops petals and lay a cocktail stick on one and then add the second on top and squeeze together and secure. Then glue and add the other two loops and arrange and shape accordingly.

Dry upside down inserted into a piece of green flower oasis or in a former right side up.

Next, make eight outer loops per flower in black paste. These should be as thin as possible. Carefully glue to the underside of the yellow inner centre and once again dry but in a former and shape.

Make the petals in a deep red paste. Construct in two phases, making the four inner petals first and affixing to the centre and then the outer four petals. There is a deliberate gap in the first central loop.

The petals on the small flower are made of three beaded rolls, the medium and large flower have four beaded rolls, but the beaded rolls for the large flower are larger.

To begin the process, dust the underside to stop the petals sticking and then add some glue to the base of the petals and to the underside of the flower centre.

Assemble carefully upside down and ensure each petal is stuck completely.

Place a former over the upside down flower and then turn the right side up.

Adjust accordingly and support the petals underneath with small pieces of kitchen roll making a slight concave shape.

Once dry add the outer layer of petals and dry once more.

The leaves are created with green paste and comprise a central double or triple loop.

The flared outer pieces are from a single beaded roll cut to shape with each piece having a point.

For the double looped leaves there is one set of side pieces, for the triple looped leaves there are either two or to form larger leaves five pieces.

Line up all the pieces and glue together and then seal and secure the base.

Arrange and shape each leaf into a flared arrangement and allow to dry for a while.

Turn the dried, flower upside down and add glue to the base of the flower and the leaves and then attach the leaves.

Poppy French Beaded Flower

Place the flower and the leaves in a former and add pieces of kitchen roll underneath the leaves to add shape and allow to dry or dry upside down.

Sunflower
French Beaded Flower

This vibrant Sunflower forms a colourful display and is made up of a dark brown, coiled centre and a variety of pointed multi-looped bright yellow petals.

The leaves are formed of individual beaded rolls glued together in various lengths.

The cake used for the flowers is a two-tier creation that would make an ideal birthday or celebration cake and could also be expanded into a wedding cake with third tier.

The cake is painted with a unique paint effect of splattering.

The white border is created using a 'knit' embossed rolling pin from Jack and Gill Crafts along with a white beaded roll at the top and bottom edge.

French Beaded Flowers in Sugar

Create the centres first. Follow the same instructions for the centre of the daisy or the gardenia or magnolia, but these centres are much bigger.

Take a truffle sized ball of dark brown paste and flatten one side. Insert a glued cocktail stick and allow to dry completely.

Make a beaded roll out of more dark brown paste and cut the end to form a point.

Glue the base and create a simple coil. Glue to the flattened cone, secure and allow to dry.

Next, make several small and thin loops out of the dark brown paste and glue carefully to the back of the centre. They only need to overlap slightly.

Then cut up a beaded roll into small pieces and soften one end of each piece and affix around the loops in two layers.

Secure and allow to dry.

There are eight petals per flower made in bright yellow paste, and they are all comprised of three layers of beaded rolls.

Each set of petals varies in size for each flower to achieve the different sized flowers.

Once formed, gently pinch the end to form a point.

Affix to the reverse of the centre upside down and allow to dry.

Make the leaves from a green beaded roll. Cut one long roll and then glue others reducing in size on either side. Affix to the reverse of each flower, shape and support with pieces of kitchen roll and allow to dry.

Peony
French Beaded Flower

Undoubtedly striking, dramatic and colourful, the Peony is a more adventurous flower and does require a lot more care and thought, but well worth it.

The flower is formed with a large arrangement of long, twisted yellow loops to construct the centre and surrounded by six large, cupped coiled petals.

There are also little buds at the base of the top tier made of small loops surrounded by small green beaded leaves.

The cake used for the flowers is a two-tier creation that would make an ideal celebration or wedding cake. For a larger cake, smaller peonies could also be made for added decoration. The cake is painted with a ragging paint effect in gold.

The gold border for the top tier is created using an ornate braiding mould that will be available via Nicholas Lodge and Katy Sue Designs. A similar alternative can be used such as the Plaited Borders mould from Karen Davies. The bottom tier is covered in gold fabric panels embossed vertically and horizontally with the largest ribbed roller and dusted in a gold lustre dust.

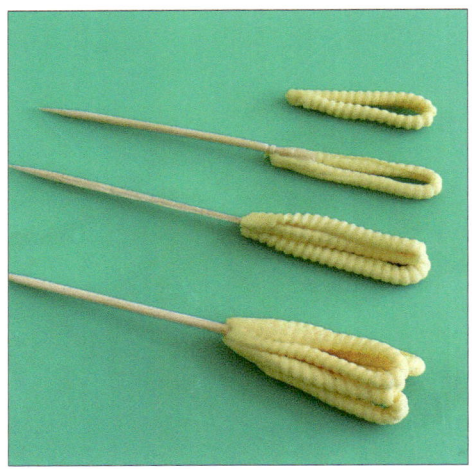

For the centre of the peony, create a core of long beaded rolls in yellow paste using the smaller of the ribbed rollers. The length should be determined by the size of the petals, so that when assembled they sit comfortably within the cupped petals. In this instance they were about 2.5" 6.5cm) long.

Take one loop and affix and glue a cocktail stick firmly.

Glue another two loops and allow to dry. Add more layers of twisted loops drying each layer. Finally, when the centre reaches a reasonable size, dry in a suitably sized funnel.

For the vibrant red petals, there are two ways to create them – one wired, one non-wired. The basic shape is the same – a large coil with additional rolls wrapped around the coil.

For the wired petal make a large coil (follow the instructions from the coiled, spiral flower project). It is also possible to form the petal with one very long beaded roll.

Particularly look at the method of making the petal bigger with the addition of a second roll if necessary.

Attach further red beaded rolls wrapped and glued around the coil, which should be about 3.5" (9cm).

Insert a glued 26g wire into the coil and secure.

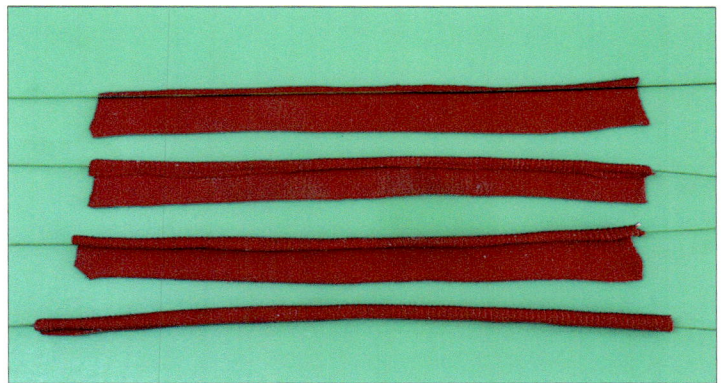

Create another final beaded roll but this time with a 26g wire glued inside and wrap around the coiled section. Secure the wire at the base with tape. Cup and shape the petal and leave to dry.

To complete the flower tape the petals around the yellow centres with an inner layer and then an outer layer of three petals.

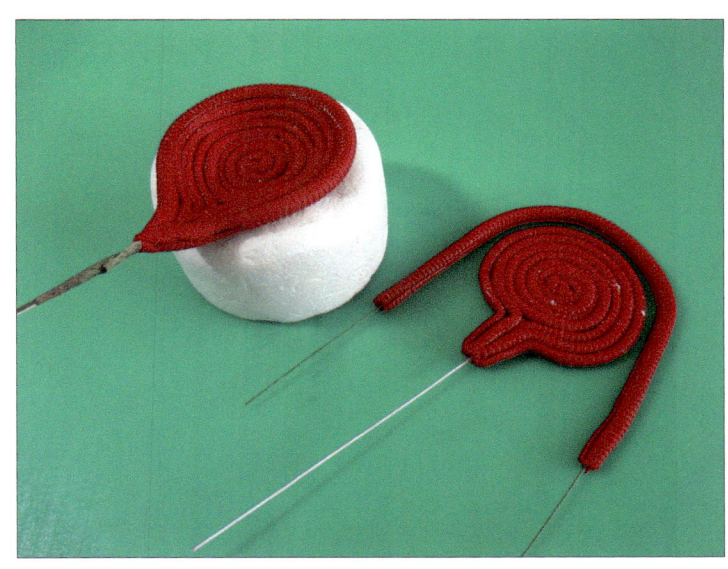

For the non-wired version make the six petals (it is best to make this with a strong paste like gelatin paste or a paste with added gum tragacanth) and add glue to the base of each petal. Place inside a small bowl sprayed with cake release. Leave to dry for several days.

Take out of the bowl and dry further upside down. Finally, attach to the top of the cake with melted white chocolate and freeze-dry with freeze ice in a can.

Make a hole in the top centre and carefully insert the twisted yellow loops.

Peony French Beaded Flower

The small bud arrangements are made of six small red loops glued to a cocktail stick surrounded by six, small, double looped, pointed green beaded leaves.

Dahlia
French Beaded Flower

Dramatic and colourful, the Dahlia is also a more adventurous French beaded flower to make, being formed of multiple layers and therefore delicate to evolve.

There is a dark red centre with vertical pointed beads surrounded by small red loops and then several layers of petals in bright orange and yellow.

This flower is complemented by an arrangement of three green leaves created with central coil and pointed beaded rolls on either side.

The cake used for the flowers is a three-tier creation that would make an ideal celebration or wedding cake.

The cake is painted with a paint effect that comprises applying a base layer of mid-cream and then hand-painted marbling.

The border is created using an ornate art deco motif mould from Karen Davies Cakes.

French Beaded Flowers in Sugar   97

First, make the flower centres and refer back to the centres made for the blue fantasy flower project. Insert a glued cocktail stick into a cone shaped piece of dark red paste and allow to dry.

Create thin, dark red beaded rolls and cut into small pieces to fit the side of the cone. Cut with one end to form a point. Add glue to the cone and affix all the pointed pieces. It is best to start by adding four pieces like dividing a circle into four, and then adding the other pieces into the gaps.

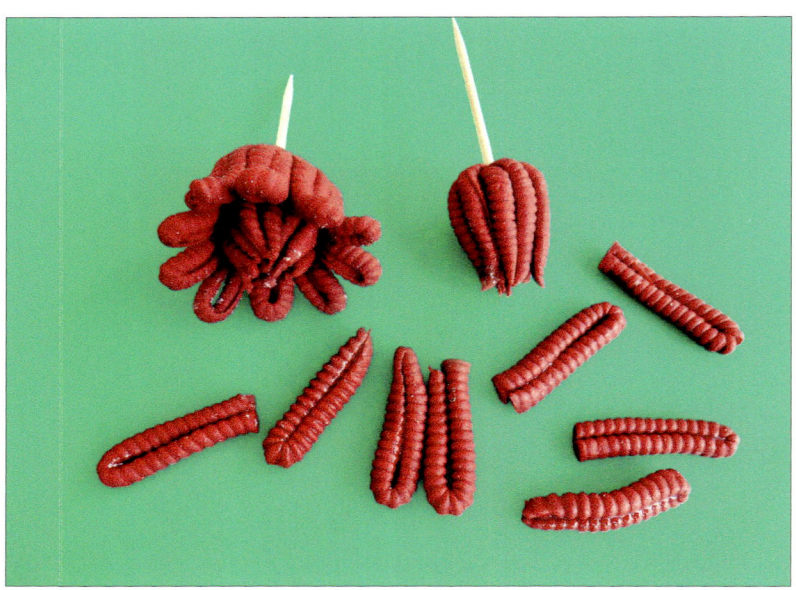

However, these pointed pieces do not neatly fit the top but all overlap and open.

Flatten to the underside of the cone and allow to dry completely.

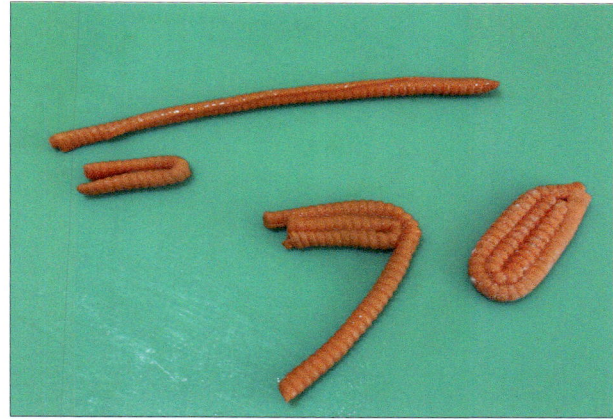

Next, create ten or eleven small loops (depending on how many can fit the centre) also in dark red paste and glued together with no gap.

Affix to the centre and arrange so they open up and dry completely.

The next layer of petals is made of bright orange paste.

For the smaller flower, there is one layer of seven double tight loops – with little or no gap. For the medium flower there is an inner layer of seven loops again and an outer layer of seven single loops. For the large flower, there is an inner and outer layer of seven double loops, and these petals are slightly larger.

The outer layer of petals are made of yellow paste. For the small flower, there are seven double loops, for the medium and large flower there are seven triple loops, but for the larger flower, the petals are larger than the medium ones.

Assemble each layer one by one and dry in a former with pieces of kitchen roll underneath the petals to give support and shape.

Each flower has three leaves of different sizes made of green paste.

The core is a glued coil that is wrapped with glued beaded rolls to form a pointed end.

Leave the leaves to dry for 10-15 minutes.

Turn the flower upside down, add glue to the underside, and to the leaf, and glue each leaf in place.

Leave to dry upside down with kitchen roll underneath to give shape.

A Range of Other French Beaded Flowers in Sugar

About the Author

Gary Chapman first developed an interest in sugarcraft in the early 90s when he worked for Merehurst Publishing, who had built up a worldwide reputation as the leading publisher of cake decorating books.

Invigorated by this exciting edible art medium, he set up Iced Delights in the early 1990s, invented the new technique of fabric effects in sugar, published his own book (Fabric Effects in Sugar) and gave demonstrations and classes all over the UK and the USA.

Over the years his innovative fabric effects in sugar ideas and techniques have become mainstream and adopted globally.

Later, he launched and became editor for the first-ever mass-market cake decorating magazine. He also produced Iced and Easy, a cake book for W.H. Smith and provided display pieces for exhibitions of edible art called 'A Taste of Art'.

After another period in publishing, he reformed Iced Delights in 1999 and became one of the top ten wedding cake makers in London.

In 2006, he left London for a quieter life in the Cotswolds where he now lives.

Email gazchappers@btinternet.com
Facebook page at :
Gary Chapman Cakes
Gary Chapman Cakes website at :
http://www.garychapmancakes.com
Edditt Publishing at :
www.eddittpublishing.com

Fabric Effects in Sugar
First Steps and Basic Skills
by Gary Chapman

Paperback £7.99 ISBN 978-1-909230-00-2
Ebook (epub) £6.99
ISBN 978-1-909230-01-9
Ebook (mobi) £6.99
ISBN 978-1-909230-02-06

How to create a range of basic fabric effects in sugar, including drapes, hangings or tails, bows, borders and flowers

Fabric Effects in Sugar Book One introduced the idea of emulating fabric effects in sugar when it was first published in 1993 and started a huge trend in cake decorating that continues unabated today. This landmark book in cake decorating has been out of print for many years and has been re-published as a revised edition for a new audience to enjoy.

Learn how to produce a range of basic fabric effects such as the drape, hangings or tails, bows, rosettes, ribbon cockade, borders and several varieties of flowers and leaves, including a fabric effect rose. All of these effects provide a simple and quick alternative to the usual methods of cake decorating and yet at the same time produce a stylish and attractive finish.

The ideas in the book can be adapted and used in conjunction with all other cake decorating techniques.

- Ten distinctive and colourful cakes.
- Black and white diagrams.
- Step by step instructions.
- Useful section on how to paint cakes.

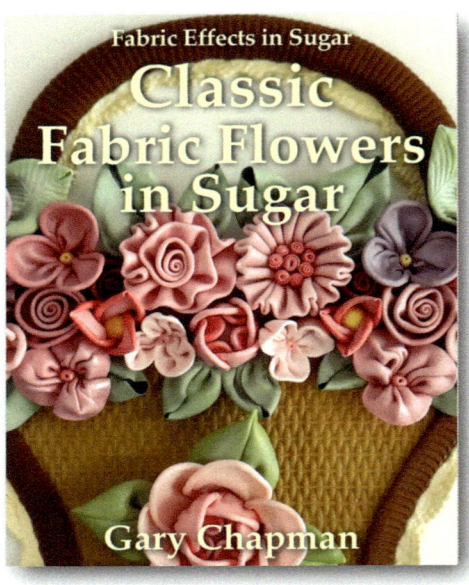

Fabric Effects in Sugar
Classic Fabric Flowers in Sugar
by Gary Chapman

Paperback £14.99 ISBN 9781909230170
Hardcover £23.99 ISBN 9781909230200
Ebook (Epub) £8.99
ISBN 9781909230187
Ebook (Mobi) £8.99
ISBN 9781909230194

A colourful step-by-step guide showing how to make a range of fabric effect flowers and leaves from roses to fantasy flowers for cakes

A natural progression from *Fabric Effects in Sugar: First Steps and Basic Skills*, *Classic Fabric Flowers in Sugar* is solely focused on how to make a range of simple fabric effect flowers and a range of leaves. All of these flowers offer a simple alternative to making the usual sugar flowers, which often take a long time to construct. These techniques are usually quicker but equally attractive.

The flowers featured include: the rolled rose, the pleated rose, a hybrid half rolled and half pleated rose, cabachon roses, simple blossom, textured and double sided blossom, patterned paste blossom, rosette flowers, pointed petalled fantasy flower, concave flower, poinsettia, Christmas rose and mistletoe.

- Fantasy inspired flowers are currently hugely popular
- Colour photography and clear instructions
- Full step by step photographs of how to make the flowers and leaves
- Includes several different types of fabric effect roses
- Describes the three essential techniques of rolling, folding and pleating
- Illustrates the techniques of double sided paste and texturing or embossing
- Shows the use of flower centres - wired and on cocktail sticks
- Includes stunning floral samplers and examples of cakes featuring fabric effect flowers
- Details many sources of inspiration
- Complements Gary Chapman's Craftsy class *Rolled Fondant Flowers*

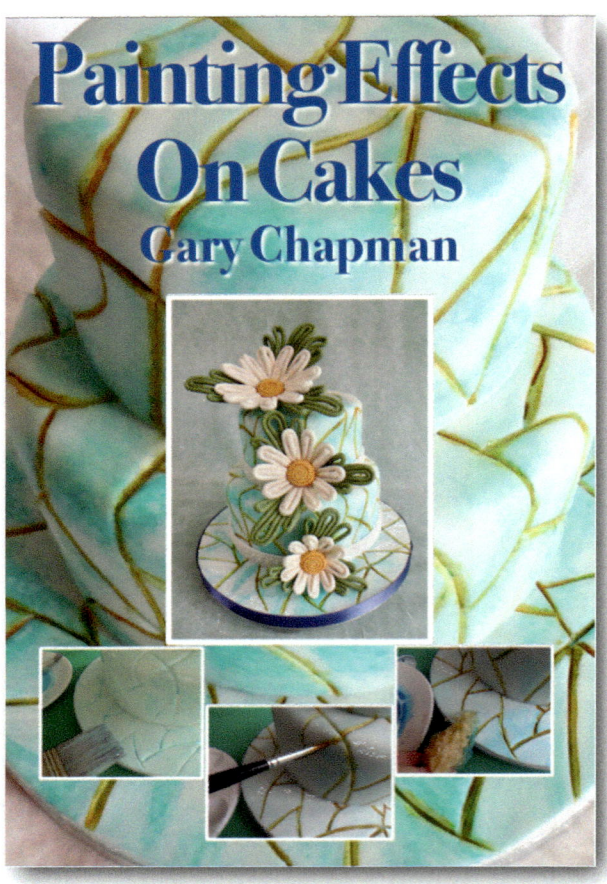

Painting Effects on Cakes by Gary Chapman

Paperback £16.99
ISBN 9781909230170

Due 2019

A colourful step-by-step guide showing how to paint cakes using traditional home decorating painting techniques such as brush strokes, flat washes, sponging, ragging, marbling, splattering, stippling, bagging and various other ideas.

I first recognised the potential of utilising traditional home decorating painting techniques for cakes in the 1990s. At the time I was working for various publishers who had a foothold in craft books and this was one of the trends we had on our radar.

I quickly utilised these techniques such as ragging, sponging, flat washing, brush strokes, splattering, stippling and marbling in my cake decorating repertoire and some featured in *Fabric Effects in Sugar: First Steps and Basic Skills*. This was the first time that these ideas had been adapted to cake decorating and since then I have given many demonstrations that incorporate these ideas.

In more recent years painting on cakes has become a hot topic and so my techniques have a greater validity and relevance today.

Most of the cakes in *French Beaded Flowers in Sugar* have been painted using some of these evocative and simple painting techniques.